MW01249241

PORTRAITS OF CHANGE

Unparalleled Freedoms,
Unanticipated Consequences

Mary White Stewart

Hamilton Books
A member of
The Rowman & Littlefield Publishing Group
Lanham · Boulder · New York · Toronto · Plymouth, UK

Copyright © 2013 by
Hamilton Books
4501 Forbes Boulevard
Suite 200
Lanham, Maryland 20706
Hamilton Books Acquisitions Department (301) 459-3366

10 Thornbury Road
Plymouth PL6 7PP
United Kingdom

Library of Congress Control Number: 2012950663
ISBN: 978-0-7618-6037-2 (paperback : alk. paper)
eISBN: 978-0-7618-6038-9

Cover photograph: The author with her mother,
St. Louis, Missouri, 1945.

This book is dedicated to my mother,
Helen Tyler Stewart
and my grandmothers
Ada Virginia White and Inez Tyler Stewart
2012

Ada Virginia White, 1891-1978

Inez Tyler Stewart, 1893-1988

Helen Tyler Stewart, 1921-

Mary White Stewart, 1945-

Tyler Mary Stewart, 1970-

Kate Stewart-Hudson, 1977-

Contents

Preface

To still the distractions of my everyday life and quiet my mind, I imagine myself in a trailer on the Paiute Indian Reservation at Pyramid Lake, Nevada. It sits in a small park a few hundred feet from the lakeshore, next to the Crosby House, a bar and general store stocked with chips, beer and vacation necessities, as well as silver and turquoise jewelry and heavily beaded moccasins. The image of this trailer merges with the small dusty towns we lived in, always hovering on the edges, the slow days dominated by waiting and watching. The trailer I see myself writing in is the very smallest Airstream, everything within arm's reach. Sometimes it is winter and I am barely warm enough to write, going from bed to teakettle and back to the heavy blankets of my bed. At other times, I sit in a folding webbed chair drinking ice tea as the day melts into evening.

Pyramid Lake, austere and mysterious, is filled with memories of my childhood in small desert towns and the gambling town of Reno, Nevada. The strongest of these memories is built around the great divide between the lives our Basque and Italian neighbors lived, centered on their farms and ranches, high school basketball, little league games and family, and a woman, outcast by all but my parents, whose life gave my sister and me hope for something besides the dreariness we saw unfolding around us.

By marvelous happenstance, our neighbor in the old railroad town of Wadsworth, Nevada was Lucille Liebling. Her marriage and divorce from well-known writers, A. J. Liebling and A. C. Spectorsky, wrapped her in a cloak of dramatic romance, mystery and sophistication. She had left New York City to settle in Wadsworth after her divorce from Liebling, ostensibly to benefit from the arid climate, but primarily to pursue her romantic image of the Wild West with its vast skies, open spaces, cowboys and Indians. She actually found the cowboys and Indians she was looking for, picking them up as they hitchhiked, in her old maroon station wagon on her way home from Reno, shocking the community when they stayed with her a few days, sometimes even a few months. She lived alone with her gregarious brown lab, Friday, in a small tarpaper covered house a few yards from the Truckee River. She sunbathed in her back yard, overgrown with lavender and herbs, completely naked, pale hair wound around thick rollers, cigarette close by, and welcomed the criticism and gossip that floated to her on the sage-drenched air.

Sometimes, on late summer afternoons she would invite my sister, Holly, and me to go with her to Pyramid Lake, the enormous, desolate saltwater remnant of a lake that once covered much of Nevada, for a swim and a picnic. She packed steaks, crusty rounds of bread, heavy red wine and cigarettes in a grocery sack, and even with the big dog lolling in the back, a rusty barbecue, and a ten-year-old station wagon, we felt like stars in a Hollywood romance as we sped across the desert. We swam in the warm salt water and spent the sunset hours absorbing the warmth of the coarse sand drying on our skin. The day slipped almost imperceptibly from a sheer white heat to a soft blanket of deep violets and blues, the musty taste of wine and cigarettes lying heavy on our tongues. Later, watching Lucille boil water for tea in her crowded kitchen, listening to her stories about New York, Europe, publishing, and men, it seemed absolutely possible that we would not always live in Wadsworth, Nevada. It began to seem absurd, knowing what we now did about men and the world, sophisticated enough even to smoke cigarettes, that we were stuck in that isolated, lifeless town abandoned on the edge of the reservation.

The deep chasm between the life Lucille showed us and the life we were living reflected the many conflicts I grew up with, personal as well as those fueled by the dramatic changes of the 1960s; conflict between the relatively privileged life my mother brought to her marriage and my father's life growing up on a farm near Sikeston, Missouri with six other children. These conflicts followed me through our move from the rural South where even the lovely Miss Sunshine Brooks, my first grade teacher, thoughtlessly tossed us racial epithets, to the West, still hovering on the periphery of the places we lived. The boredom and weariness I felt as a girl stuck looking after the younger kids while our parents spent long days picking apricots and peaches in the fields collided with the girl I imagined myself to be, riding my outlaw horse, hiding out in the dusty bushes lining the road to home. And the discord came to be between the self and identity, the interior struggles and the public face, the demands for perfection and the desire for authenticity. But the clashes that most deeply affected me, changed my world, were between the secure and stable 1950s and the disrupted, uncertain decades that followed, transforming my life, and eventually the whole country. The transformation for me, while not from skinny kid living in a ragged desert town to a Hollywood starlet, was almost as great—from a girl bound by a sure knowledge that her future was as a wife and mother to a woman whose future was uncharted, open, exhilarating and fraught with the potential for missteps and mistakes. The roiling changes brought to me and millions of young women by the women's movement swept us into a world of unexpected pleasures and pains, of choice, opportunity, and freedoms our mothers and grandmothers could not have dreamed of. And the lives we lived, sometimes soaring, sometimes stumbling, laid a foundation for our daughters that was equally unforeseeable.

My grandmothers, my mother, my daughters, like I, like all of us, lived a day at a time, too occupied with the demands of work, children, husbands, lovers and friends to be able to frame their lives with historical or social meaning. But, when I look at these lives, the ways they fold together and veer apart, I see the enormous paradoxes created by progress, the fissures created by change, both the darkness and light of freedoms hard won. Standing back from these lives, taking the long view of the past, allows me to see how our lives, and the lives of generations of women, are both woven together and widely separated by the experiences we shared. This helps me disentangle the many threads of joy and despair my daughters and I have shared, caused one another, and from which we have built our identities, our relationships and our lives.

This book grew from my efforts, both as a sociologist and a woman, to clarify my own life, to make sense of the deep conflicts between all the freedom the women's movement brought and the unanticipated costs of these freedoms, the fissures between the openness and opportunity and the demands and damage they sometimes brought, between the thoughtless and cavalier way I rushed through the rapidly changing world and the long term impact of the decisions I made on my daughters. I wrote about these because I knew I was not the only woman who had these experiences, these confusing, exhilarating conflicts between what I had grown up expecting and what I could now have. A social movement is not an abstraction, not only an historical fact—we who lived it were irrevocably changed by it, for better and for worse, and I thought my life and the closely tied lives of four generations of women in my family could illuminate the powerful personal impact of a political movement.

Acknowledgments

Thank you, my grandmothers, Ada Virginia White and Inez Tyler Stewart, for letting me spend days with you talking about things so personal you probably never imagined anyone would ask about them. You tolerated your young, new Ph.D. granddaughter intruding into your private lives over three decades ago, refusing me only when I stepped too far into your pain. My daughters, Tyler and Kate, I thank you for talking to me about experiences that were enormously difficult for you, and for me, and for being strong enough to share them—without you this work would have been incomplete. And my mother, Helen Stewart, you will not understand this book, you will not remember that I have written it, or that the difference between your life and mine was the impetus for it, but you are on every page.

I began this book while on sabbatical from the University of Nevada, Reno, and without that time away and alone I could not have started this work. I want to thank my friends and colleagues who have read, re-read, criticized and offered hope as I wrote this book over the last ten years. I especially want to thank Pat Gallagher, who not only helped me with syntax and tense, and kept me honest, but who has been my dear and supportive friend and my children's second mother and mainstay throughout their lives. My colleague, Rosemary Dixon, helped me keep the story coherent and buoyed my spirits by telling me parts of this were "beautiful," even when I was at my most self-critical. Thank you, my friend and colleague, Larry Reynolds, for providing encouragement and support that nurtured and validated me as I wrote this book, and throughout my career.

Sincere and heartfelt thanks to my daughter Tyler who read early drafts, who challenged my interpretations and refreshed my memories and who filled the margins of my manuscript with so many insightful, helpful comments I almost despaired. And, thanks to my daughter Kate for making me justify or change one word or one phrase far more often than I wished, for enriching my language and expanding my thoughts, and whose thoughtful editing helped make this book, finally, the book I wanted to write.

Introduction

The high-spirited, smoking, drinking, boyishly dressed and bobbed young women known as flappers ushered in the1920s, dancing the Charleston and the Black Bottom, drinking gin fizzes and martinis at speakeasies, driving cars and riding bicycles, enjoying petting parties and sex before marriage, and in general, joyfully flaunting the heavy constraints of the social norms of their day. Although their exuberance couldn't survive the heavy losses of the Great Depression and the stock market crash, this brief shining moment was to reappear forty years later. This time, these pivotal shifts from one set of social expectations to another were to affect not just the few and the very young, but to dramatically alter the lives of an entire generation of women and to substantially shape the lives of their daughters and granddaughters. The life we had been preparing for, filling our hope chests with tea towels and tablecloths, reading romance comics and movie magazines and dreaming of weddings and babies, was suddenly undone by the knowledge that we could create ourselves completely anew. While we had been convinced of the importance of saving ourselves for our future husbands, knowing, of course, that marriage was a given, after birth control pills became widely available in the early 1960s, we could have sex with relative abandon, even though we still weren't totally unconcerned with whether he would respect us in the morning. While we had been dreaming about whom we would marry, that is, who we would finally *be,* now we faced the thrilling, frightening possibility that we could *be* on our own. While we had imagined ourselves working for a few years as a nurse or secretary to put our husbands through law school or medical school, we could now see ourselves pursuing those dreams. How would all this choice and freedom affect us? How thoughtful were we about the consequences of our choices, about what we were giving up? And how prepared were we for the new?

We grabbed opportunities for change though we had no preparation for the consequences of our decisions. Before the decade of the 1960s was over, the lives of ordinary women would change drastically, in ways that we never would have imagined and with an impact felt today in ongoing political and social fissures. Of course, in part we just grew up and the changes we went through were those of my mother's generation and her mother's: finishing school, falling in love, getting married, working, having children, growing old. But our generation of women found all of these transitions redefined, fraught with conflicting meaning, the availability and consequences of choices being far different than they had been just a generation before. This book is about these experiences, and their shifting meanings, inextricably tied to time and place.

In this book I pull the lives of my grandmothers and mother into the stream of life my daughters and I have lived during a time of dramatic change, especially for women, in this country. When I was in high school, "the sixties" had not yet begun in Wadsworth, Nevada where I lived, or in any other small town in this country. We listened to the longings of Rosemary Clooney and at the same time played with paper dolls of her, dressing her for dates and gardening. We spent long hours with Hank Williams and Frankie Avalon, the Shangri-Las and Little Richard, and swooned over the romances of Tab Hunter, Doris Day and Audrey Hepburn. The movie magazines we read revealed lives beyond our reach, and while we loved the stories about romance and loss, those lives weren't our own. A generation earlier my mother had joined her friends to worship at the altar of Frank Sinatra whose love songs lulled them into marriages with soldiers, handsome in their starched uniforms, leaving on dangerous missions to return as heroes, if they did return. My daughters' music was harder, rougher, preparing them for a harsher adolescence navigating the omnipresent pull of drugs, sex and alcohol that was far more powerful than what my generation had experienced, preparing them for an adulthood defined as laden with heavy responsibility rather than the freedoms adulthood had promised us.

We can see the impact of any social or historical period by tracing its influence on individual, situated lives, recognizing that one's social and economic location provides shape to the rather fluid boundaries of these lives. Looking carefully, and critically, at these lives as they are situated within time and place can illustrate the enormous changes that took place in women's lives as they experienced, so very differently, the "same" events. Our experiences, tightly woven into the mundane demands and expectations of everyday life, reveal a pattern as they are constructed and contextualized in a social climate that shifts with each generation. The experiences of marriage, divorce, raising children, suffering through their perilous and destructive choices, making painful decisions about work and family, dealing with loss, and enduring depression and feelings of worthlessness are not unique to this writer. Pulling these experiences from their place in everyday life and unraveling them for our scrutiny, however, can reveal them as reflections of a particular moment in this country's history in which women's lives, and consequently the lives of those they loved, were dramatically and irreversibly changed.

This book is about what I understand as shared experience—not shared by everyone who was a young woman like I was as the women's movement began to undo the comfort and constraints of the 1950s, but shared in large part by hundreds of thousands of us. Though we tell stories about the same events, such as marriage and divorce, events so commonplace that they are taken for granted in our lives, our experiences of them are very different. While anyone my age couldn't help but be caught up in the drama and tragedy of the war in Viet Nam, each of us experienced it differently, some eagerly signing up to fight, some being caught in crossfire and dying in Southeast Asia, others demonstrating against the war in college towns across the country. We experienced something our children have not known, but we didn't all have the same experience. By the same token, while the Second World War may have shaped my parents' marriage and early years together, and while Betty Freidan and Barbara Ehrenreich are no doubt right about the sweeping patterns of change that took place in the economy and in relationships between couples after the war, each person constructed these changes differently. My grandmothers lived in completely different worlds, only fifty miles apart; my mother's mother living in relative ease in Bonne Terre, Missouri, even during the Depression, married to the minister of the town's biggest church, a man she loved and fought to keep; my father's mother bound to a loveless marriage of obligation and hardship, married to a dour and bitter farmer in the boot heel of Missouri, her greatest happiness coming in the last decade of her life when she was completely alone. My parents' longing for love and safety at the beginning of WW II forged a marriage fractured by deep differences in values and expectations, roped together by hope and romance, and finally, just by necessity. These lives are at the head-waters of the stream into which I pull my own life and that of my daughters as we share the outlines of experiences that are colored so very differently. The lives of four generations of women, connected by the tough, silken threads of family, spanning over one hundred years, illustrate the enormous changes that occurred during a period of marvelous new freedoms and reveal the unanticipated, often painful consequences they produced.

I
Constructing Childhood

I saved my daughters' hair from the time I first cut their bangs and from the time they first dyed their naturally dark locks to shocking blondes and reds. I saved their pink and yellow swirled birthday candles, their smocked dresses and tights, their first leather shoes, and their first bras and high heels. I saved their dolls and their books, and it is only lately that I feel some detachment from these things that, for me, held the meaning of their childhoods. I might have thought I was just packing memories away for them, but really I saved these things as much to prove that I was a good, caring mother doing the right things in their lives, as I did for them to someday have these pieces of their childhoods. I was keeping a record for myself of the ways I provided, confirming to myself that being a single, working mother did not indicate my girls were going to receive a second-rate childhood. I was safeguarding against implications that they were being somehow deprived, against hints that what I could offer my children was inferior and deficient. The proof was there in the artifacts I saved from their first Christmases, first haircuts, first steps, first words, and first grade.

I have no dolls, no books, no dresses from my childhood, a clear indication to me when I was a young mother stockpiling evidence of my mothering abilities, that my mother was more distracted, less involved, really just not as good a mother as I was determined to be. Now I think maybe my mother didn't need these assurances. She may have felt more authentic in her daily life as a mother and didn't need to rely on ritual markers to prove she was there with her children or that they were there with her. Maybe she didn't have the energy or interest needed to pack up all the mementos of five childhoods each time we moved. I was born only fifteen months after my brother Johnny, the oldest, and then Holly, my younger sister, arrived in less than three years. Stewart followed soon thereafter, then Geoff. By the time my mother was thirty she had given birth to all five of her children, so perhaps the actual presence of all of us outweighed anything we drew or wore or received. Clothes and toys and books were handed down from one of us to the next, so they were too frayed and worn by the time the last child had finished with them to think of saving them.

My mother saved photographs and letters, words and stories, not things. She made photo albums for each of us, choosing those photos that included us with friends and family, or that marked our graduations or trips or weddings. She made us books of letters from her father, letters from us while we were away at camp or graduate school, letters from her sisters when they were young mothers after WW II. She saved the letters her father sent her when she went to college, one of which I have framed on my dresser: "Helen, here is $1.00 for the week. I wish I could send more. Love, Dad."

I learned much of what I know about how my mother and grandmothers' felt about their childhoods by collecting their oral histories years ago. My grandmother White's recollection of her childhood reflected the harsh conditions of her life, a life made more difficult by the fact that both of her parents died when she was a child, leaving her dependent on the good will of her mother's brother and his wife. Her name was Ada Virginia, but her grandkids called her "Mom." Death of a parent was not at all unusual in the early 1900s, just as parents could almost anticipate losing a child in infancy, as my grandmothers did. When a mother died, her sister often took her place, or the father remarried to provide a new mother for his children and a helpmeet for himself. Mom recalled:

> I had to go live with my aunt when she got married, and my uncle was just as hateful as he could be. He used to whip me with his wagon whip, buggy whip, or anything. I remember him lickin' me so many times. The thing I hated most in the world is he'd say, 'Ada, go in there and get a pan of water and come wash my feet and dry them' and I had to do it or I got a whippin'. It made me feel like a slave. I still remember how that made me feel.
>
> When I was a little bitty child, just seven, he'd make me go to the field by myself. I had to pick and hoe cotton and if I didn't pick just so much he'd whip me at night. Once, he whipped me with a razor strop, and I just run off to live with another aunt until my aunt made him promise he wouldn't whip me and I just went on back. When he was old and sick for so long, and dying, I would go up and visit him at the hospital—carry things to him. He must have forgotten how mean he was all his life. He'd cry and I felt sorry for him and sorry for the way I had felt all my life about him. But I never did love him.
>
> All the children had to mind more than children today and work more, but I think it was harder for us orphan children. 'Course, when I was born, we didn't have so much as people do today and we didn't expect so much either. I was the baby, but my mother died when I was just nine months old. My father tried to

raise us kids up and he kept us until he died when I was about four. Then I was taken to live with my uncle and his wife. Even though she was just my aunt by marriage, she treated me a lot better than my own blood relatives did. He was the meanest thing there ever was.

Mom's childhood was distinguished by work, tedium, and what today would be called child abuse. My grandmother worked from the time she could look after the younger children or carry a cotton sack on her shoulder.

I had to work for my aunt because I was the oldest; four years older than her oldest, so I understand why she made me help out. She used to put a pan down on a chair for me to wash the dishes. I can see now why she needed me and why she taught me the things she done, and I never did hold anything she ever done against her, I don't think. When we was little, we did play some, but mostly, especially when we got older, there was always something to do, work all the time, work, no play. Work. Mostly in the fields, either to chop cotton stalks, knock them down, or chop corn stalks and pick them up and pile and burn them if we wasn't picking cotton. It was just slave labor and all the children there was raised that way.

None of this description of a joyless and difficult childhood was accompanied by self-pity or an expectation of appreciation or understanding. She was just remembering, from the more comfortable distance of seventy years or so. She didn't mention any pretty clothes or toys. She took whatever her aunt and uncle would allow her and asked for nothing more. Her expectations for love and marriage grew out of this rocky, undernourished soil.

Her husband's, my grandfather Pop's, life as a child was no easier than hers had been.

Pop had a hard childhood too. His mother had nine children, three husbands, three children by each husband. Her last husband and she was separated and all the kids stayed with his mother. Pop had to work in a cotton mill from the time he was just a little boy. He was working all the time in the cotton mills in Alabama and Georgia and Mississippi and Tennessee. The family moved a lot and all the children had to work in the cotton mills. Pop always was stooped from that kind of work.

When I visited with my grandmother Inez Stewart, we sat in the solid, graceful chairs she had since her children were young and she painted a picture of a childhood completely unlike that of my grandmother White. She told of a happy, breezy childhood in the small town of DuQuoin, Illinois, during which she helped with light household chores, but was not expected to, or really allowed to, work to help support the family. My mother's mother came to know hard work only after she was married and raising five children during the Depression. Her childhood, while not privileged, was easy and graceful, preparing her for marriage and motherhood. As she got older, she wanted to work, to model or "work downtown in an office," but her brothers, she said, absolutely refused to allow it. Women were to work only if they had no other choice—were widowed or poor, like my grandfather's mother, who had run a boarding house to support her family after her husband died.

> *We kids of course couldn't do just anything we pleased, although my father was a socialist and the most liberal man in DuQuoin, and sure a lot more liberal than my friends' dads. We'd go to parties and movies, go out for Cokes and just hang around. We'd get around a piano and sing, have yard parties, make cake and ice cream. None of us worked. There wasn't much for us to do; girls could either teach until they got married, or clerk or work in someone else's home. Girls just didn't work, although once I got an offer to model shoes for a department store. My mother and brothers put their foot down on that—a girl's place was in the home with her mother. Women we knew didn't work unless they taught or clerked or worked for someone else at home if they had to. So that didn't seem like anything I wanted to do. And none of the girls in my group planned to go on to college either. Some of the boys did, and of course your grandfather did. He was the smartest man I knew—had to be to go to Harvard.*

Inez's father restlessly pursued one financially risky endeavor after another, and was never very successful at any of them, but despite his misfortunes, her own life seemed little affected.

> *My mother had been a beautiful girl and my father was a big, happy man. They had us three children, first Fred and William, then me, pretty quick. They seemed to get off to such a good start in life, but it seemed like my Dad's luck turned from bad to worse with each new venture. First, he sank a coal mine and there was no coal, or was it oil? Then he started a saw mill and that fell apart for some reason, and then he was a butcher for a while. For ten years before he died, he ran a neighborhood grocery store. But even with all of that, he was happy, always giving the kids who came into the store candy, and joking with them, especially the girls. He was only fifty-nine, and my mother was ten years younger, when he died.*
>
> *We girls just palled around together. We played in the streets, which was pretty safe because they weren't paved and there were no cars. We played "skip to my lou" and other games, and got together to make taffy and fudge. My mother and the other mothers generally stayed home with the children and sat on the front porch and talked and watched us kids when their work was done in the evening. The men didn't seem to be home much, at least in Du Quoin where I grew up. They came home for supper and then went to the saloon.*

Her childhood friendships laid the groundwork for the central place friends played in her life as a wife and mother. My own mother, Helen, complained that her mother's friends and their children were often more important to her than her own. She remembered her mother giving away a beautiful quilt, one of the only things she wanted for herself, to one of her friend's daughters, and sewing new school dresses for her friend Callie's girls. But, she says, the girls in her family always had at least three clean, ironed dresses in the closet for school days, and two pairs of shoes polished ritualistically by her father every Saturday afternoon.

We lived on Carroll Acres which was one of several large farms near Treze-vant, Carroll County, Tennessee for about five years. There were thousands of laying hens on the farm my dad managed, and sometimes my father took my six-year old brother, Johnny, with him to Nashville to deliver the eggs. My dad usually went alone on these overnight trips, so being invited to accompany my dad made Johnny edgy with importance. I remember there being a lot of cotton growing in those parts. I can recall the smell of the soil as I walked with my dad through cotton fields, and the heaviness of the gunny sack full with cotton that my dad sometimes let me drag. I was too little to be of any real help, but I liked feeling like his partner.

We watched the hens grow from the newly hatched chicks delivered to our house in brown cardboard boxes with symmetrical holes cut out on all sides. The boxes thrilled us—packed tightly with the noisy, warm, softness of their tiny yellow occupants. We were modern chicken farmers, the food and water constantly moving on a conveyor belt, the hens elevated in cages in a huge, concrete-floored, tempera-ture-controlled henhouse, their feet never touching the ground. Today my mother laughs at the expense of eggs from "cage free" hens. My parents had done everything possible to keep the hens indoors and off the dirty ground. She shot them full of antibiotics, plucked the dead ones from the cages, fed and watered them, and collected their eggs. She candled these eggs, separating the fertile ones from the infertile, grading and sizing them, and packing them into the boxes my brother had shaped from the flat, porous cardboard pieces stacked by the work table.

Almost twenty-five years later my sister, Holly, and I, with my five-year old daughter, Tyler, drove to Tennessee from Kansas City where I was teaching at the University of Missouri, to reconnect with Carroll Acres, the house, the town, and the feelings we believed we had carried with us through many other houses and farms and towns. We wanted to see if there were memories that survived outside of the photo albums and family nostalgia. We wanted to compare our fixed and stable visions of our past with the reality of that place and time, to tie the names of roads and neighbors, the half-memories of the house on Carroll Acres and the shops in McKenzie, with what really existed outside of our own imaginations. We sang and talked all the way from Kansas City to the chicken farm, entertaining Tyler with the folk songs and gospel tunes my parents had sung to us as children. On the trips we took across country to visit relatives in Missouri, or when we moved from Tennessee to Washington and from town to town in Washington and Nevada, the five of us kids, sometimes a dog, and my parents, all crushed into a Studebaker or Ford as we drove on highways and roads that seemed endless. We listened to my parents talk and we played games that involved the road signs and the colors and makes of cars we passed. But what really passed the time was our singing. My parents harmonized on songs I later taught my daughters; *Red River Valley, You are My Sunshine, Tennessee Waltz, Blue Hawaii, and From the Halls of Montezuma* in honor of my dad's military experience. We loved the soulful rhythm of gospel songs our parents taught us. In fact, I don't remember being really taught any song; they were just a part of our world, part of the soundtrack of our childhood that was always present in the background, taken for granted and familiar. *I've Got a Home in Glory Land* and *The Old Rugged Cross* are my favorites. Holly had the best voice, but Johnny offered a pretty strong harmony along with my mother. We were great around Christmas time.

Holly, Tyler and I found Carroll Acres at the close of a tiring day. The little shed near the side of the parched, grey house was still and dark just as it had been when I was five years old, standing at the open door, breaking the darkness to watch my brother candle eggs. The house was smaller than it had been when we lived there, and the lane leading to the neighbor's was not nearly as long as I had remembered. It was no longer threatening, densely lined with dark trees that hid insects or snakes. The hollyhock bush that stood by the front door still bloomed and we made the little dolls with swirled ruby and pink skirts that we had made every summer we lived there. Those summers were hot and dusty and we spent most of the time outside on the swing, eating crackers and drinking Kool-Aid. The days were largely unformed, foggy, only sporadically highlighted by a remembered event. I remember posing for a portrait one time, running in the house every half hour or so to sit very still on the kitchen table while mother transferred oil paint to the canvas, squinting at me, never talking until she let me go again.

My sister and I found little connection with the place we had lived. The once-familiar towns we traveled through held surprisingly few memories for us. They were unfamiliar and too quiet, the roads dusty, and the farms dreary and tired looking. That trip we made to Tennessee did not so much allow us to re-collect memories as it left us with the realization that so few had survived outside of the photo albums and family reminiscences that had constructed them.

In McKenzie, Tennessee, where Holly, Stewart and Geoffrey, my three younger siblings, were born, I sat awkwardly in the front seat of our car, my little sister standing on the seat between my dad and me. He was leaning out the window a little bit to talk to one of the neighbors, urging Holly, who was about three, to recite the poem he had taught her. She did so, softly and self-consciously: "Roses on my shoulders, slippers on my feet, I'm daddy's little darling, don't you think I'm sweet?" The rest of us sitting in the car knew she was indeed "daddy's little darling," and at the same time, it didn't really make much difference to us if we weren't. It was like saying she had on a red dress rather than a blue one. I already knew that being daddy's favorite, being special, had a down side.

Most of the memories we carried with us were built around family crises: my brother Johnny cutting his knee on an old glass telephone insulator while we were playing a jumping game, getting whipped with a willow switch by my father for trying to swim in the cow trough, the thrill of a rattle snake sliding onto the side porch where my dad hacked it to death with a hoe and hung in on the clothesline like a trophy, riding my bike over the side of the yard and hitting the road a few feet below with a terrible and painful jolt.

Sitting in the back of the schoolroom, which I remember as dark and bare, I folded the grainy lined paper on which I wrote my name for the first time and slipped it between pages in my workbook, saving it to show my mother that afternoon. Miss Sunshine would have been so happy to see it, relieved, but my shame at being the last to conquer what seemed to come so easily to the rest of the class kept me from showing her. My grandmother had cut my hair just before school started, leaving the bangs short and uneven, and I spent the first week of school stealing glances at my wavy reflection in the glass doors of a cabinet near my desk. My goals were pretty much limited to hoping my bangs would grow and hoping I didn't miss the bus home. Years later, playing 7-Up at recess or swinging alone on the playground, my goals in school hadn't grown much past getting to the right room on time, not being called on to answer a question, and finding my locker and the right bus. If we had stayed longer in one town, or started school in September along with the other kids instead of two or three months later, I may not have focused so much on my differentness, my separateness. Perhaps, if I hadn't felt so disconnected and detached from each new school with unfamiliar hallways, new peers and new teachers, my energies would have turned to reading or learning math, but as it was they were tightly wound around not being lost or left.

I was only five when we left Tennessee and moved to Washington where my dad managed another farm for a while. My mother wanted us out of the schools in rural Tennessee where even the lovely Miss Sunshine Brooks, my first grade teacher, referred to blacks as "niggers" and where racism was sewn into the fabric of everyday life.

The idea of class was never articulated by my family, but by third or fourth grade it was clear that the teachers liked some of the kids best, those who had clean lined paper and store-bought book covers instead of covers made out of grocery sacks. They brought their lunch in little crisp paper sacks made explicitly for school lunches, a new one every single day. Others of us had the wrong color writing paper, brought greasy sandwiches in newspapers or old grocery bags, and wore our socks two or three days in a row. Becoming aware of my differences, and the significance of the contrast between kids who clearly fit in and those who did not, nourished my already well-developed self-consciousness and insecurity. It made me pull in, shrink back, not raise my hand, not want to go to the board, or call out to someone across the room. It made me feign disinterest in my surroundings, and to be on time and find a seat toward the back of the classroom. Knowing the right answer to a question was a defense against the humiliation of being called on, but not knowing the answer, which was just as likely, made me shrink with shame.

We didn't talk about these feelings at home, either to each other or to our parents. Any acknowledgment that we felt inferior to anyone hit my father as a condemnation of him, his bitter response reflecting the tight constraints on feelings and expression passed down through generations in his family. My great-grand-father White had come to what he thought would be the welcoming warmth of America's South from Wales early in his life with an uncle, finding work in factories and cotton gins when he was still a boy. My grandfather White, who we called Pop, followed his father into the cotton gins, and by the time I knew him he was bent and stooped from laboring over the looms all day. From a childhood of relentless work, my grandfather became dour and hopeless before he was twenty-five. He trusted no one and needed no one outside his family. My grandmother White, Mom, whose own mother, Belle, had died when she was an infant, heard him say he loved her on their wedding day and on the day he died, and during the fifty-odd years in between, he never expressed his love to her and she didn't have any reason to believe he did. They had a working relationship; sharecropping and then farming all of their lives, raising three daughters and four sons, none of whom stayed on the farm or ever missed it.

The gloom that settled over my grandfather White was passed on as joylessness to my father, who found relief from malaise only with drink, and then only for the first few. He soon became maudlin, then mean, and finally sick before he went to bed and slept it off. My father never missed work from drinking too much, but because of it, the family was often uneasy during holidays and other important times. We didn't know if he would be drunk or get drunk at any moment, which nourished a feeling of impending danger and unpredictability. Special occasions were laced with a thin veneer of fear, an edginess that he might begin to drink and then the order would disappear. If he came to a football game, we immediately checked his sobriety. If he picked us up at a school function, we cautiously assessed the wisdom of getting in the car with him. All of us, except Holly, found ways to avoid my dad's derisive remarks, predictable and expected only when he'd had too much to drink. Hearing Dad come home late from the bar, Holly would get up and make him some eggs and toast. She would stay up and talk with him until he got tired and went to bed. There was no question that Holly was my dad's favorite, but I felt relief more than envy.

A year or so before he died, I asked my father what he wanted in the next five years, a question designed to move him from his preoccupation with death as much as to discover his plans. With no hesitation, he produced the desire to make another million dollars. I am looking at a photo of him when he was younger than I am now, maybe forty-five. A couple of strands of sandy hair blow across his forehead, he stands in a field, khaki arms folded over one another, bottom lip fuller than I ever remember, sweetly challenging the camera. He left for work early every day, reconnecting with my mother for coffee or lunch at home if he could, and always came home for supper. He seemed vaguely interested in us, particularly if there was a problem he could exacerbate by teasing or by offering irritated predictions of failure, but he seemed to see us as part of the background noise, undifferentiated, merged with one another and with place. We were his children, a block of heavy but not unpleasant responsibility. His days were spent walking irrigation ditches, sampling soil, and advising farmers on planting and rotating crops, helping them conserve the resources on which they depended. His mind was on the simple pleasure of getting rich.

By the time my father made a great deal of money, renting his trailers and apartments to people like those we had grown up with, we had all left home. I believe that the thing he most appreciated about becoming wealthy, and perhaps the reason he worked so hard to be wealthy, was simply to "show them." Over a decade ago, when he was in his late seventies, he drove his new, gold Cadillac from Nevada to Washington just to show his former boss, who had fired him thirty years before, how successful he had become.

My mother's parents never took the children anywhere if they could leave them home. Vacation was an idea whose time hadn't yet come when my parents were children. It was not until we had moved across country, far from any of our relatives, that traveling to see them became vacation time for us. I don't know how enjoyable traveling with five fidgety children in the backseat of a hot car could have been for my parents, but it was the only way we could make the trip to see the family that remained so important to both of my parents. And once there, all of us were thrilled to see the many cousins we barely knew, have picnics, water fights, listen to the grown-ups talk, catch fireflies in jars, and play outside until bedtime, settling into makeshift beds on the living room floor and talking until we fell asleep. We organized ourselves for endless family pictures because someone always seemed to have been missed the time before. I felt the dangerous excitement of visiting my cousins, Billy Joe, Kyle, and Jimmy, in a town that had no paved roads, where the signs on the service station drinking fountains specified "whites only" or "colored." Our cousins drove us around town and through the "colored section," where I felt shame for being there, for intruding, but thrilled to see a place completely inaccessible to me, the chalky unpaved roads marking the distance between my world and theirs. I helped my grandmother with her flowers, mostly watched her really, while she picked and thinned and weeded. When I see a zinnia or peony today, I am once again a skinny ten-year-old wearing shorts and a ruffled white midriff top, standing in the yard with her as she stoops over the brilliant hues in her flower beds.

On these long trips we usually stopped at a grocery store along the way where mother got the makings for a picnic lunch, bologna or peanut butter and banana sandwiches on white bread, and fruit, transforming the picnic into a celebration. We spread out a blanket in a field, or under a tree near the road, asking permission of the farmer or whoever else was around. Only one time, when we were going to split open a watermelon one late, warm afternoon and eat it under some farmer's tree, were we refused, but this refusal redefined us, turning our picnic into an intrusion, our family into undesirables. A few times a day we stopped for gas and for my parents to get coffee while we played near the car and used the bathrooms. Coffee was not a drink like tea or Coke or Kool-Aid. It was something adults had to have, like air or food.

Motels were just beginning to be popular in the fifties, and were not on the cross-country highways we traveled. We stayed overnight in hotels. Walking into the grand lobby, carpeted in plush maroon with gold swirls, the light from chandeliers dancing above, encircled by the cherry paneled walls, we were hushed with excitement. Approaching the polished wood desk with my father and listening while he arranged a room for all of us, I was always relieved when they let us in. We rode up to our room in gated and mirrored elevators, slept in beds with both a bottom and a top sheet, bedspreads and pillows, took turns in bathtubs, using tiny soaps wrapped in paper, and didn't have to share a towel. Unbelievably enough someone else cleaned the bathtub and made the bed, although I always hung up the towels and made the bed myself so they wouldn't think we had bad manners. At breakfast in the hotel dining room, chandeliers sparkling overhead, white table-cloths smoothed beneath our porcelain bowls and silver spoons, we selected cold cereal in individual foil-lined boxes, each with our own little ceramic pitcher of milk and real orange juice. Why my father ordered eggs and bacon, which we all knew he could, and did, have almost every day of his life at home was beyond us. I imagined no better future than being able to spend my life around such luxury, wearing a smart uniform and carrying keys and supplies, tidying and polishing and fluffing pillows.

In preparation for these trips, Mother got sturdy underwear boxes from J. C. Penney's or Sears, planning for two changes of clothes, a pair of pajamas, and some clean underwear and socks that would last across country. She remembers with great fondness her five children carrying these little cardboard boxes through the hotel lobby, never once thinking we would be judged badly, or at all.

* * *

Heck Road ran by our house in Prosser, Washington. It was a dry asphalt road, rimmed with milkweed and ragweed, disappearing into a plowed field planted with grapes, irrigated by small ditches running through the dusty soil. The fields Heck Road ran through were heavy with goldenrod to which my minister grandfather was terribly allergic. He walked that road with me, maybe only once, bringing with him the smell of cigars and St. Louis, letting me know that believing in God was completely my choice. "Bless this food to the nourishment of our bodies and feed our souls on the bread of life" my mother's father offered when he visited, no matter where we lived, and connected us with something more than each other at that kitchen table. We were made powerful by the union of our souls with something as warm and generous as "the bread of life." This memory is intertwined with an emerging awareness of freedom and the fear of being alone and separate in a family of people who were my whole world, and at the same time almost complete strangers.

My dad drove a tractor with a wagon hitched to the back. Those of us who were old enough walked behind and picked up rocks, throwing them in the wagon. He dumped them on the side of the field and together we built a rock fence. We sometimes helped him irrigate as he hoed new ditches, plugging up the old ones and directing the water straight down the rows cleared for grapes. Mother and Johnny planted row after row of grapes while dad was away at military camp during the summer. The bare grape sticks were taken from the bucket, stuck upright in holes dug about three feet apart, the earth pulled around them and firmly patted down. The grapes struggled in the rocky soil, Mother and Johnny watering by hand when there was a problem with the irrigation, which there often was. They were ultimately defeated by the lack of water and the dusty soil, the dry sticks stuck in little piles of dirt. By the time my Dad came home, all the grapes had died.

But the garden my mother planted thrived, row after row of ruby tomatoes, white corn, cucumbers, squash and peas. Mother spent hours hoeing and raking and weeding, while Holly and I ironed, cleaned, and seemed to be continually rearranging what little furniture we had.

My middle childhood, the softly fragmented preparation for the rapid force of change that would come a little more than a decade later, was spent on Heck Road. I was kept out of school the first year we lived on Heck Road for several months because of what I vaguely understood as "nervousness," chiefly characterized by my firm belief that my eyes and fingers were sticking together, requiring constant wide-eyed blinking and careful spreading of my fingers to unglue them. School felt like time away from the safety of home, everyone a stranger, and I was happy to see Johnny and Holly walk across the field to catch the bus without me.

Heck Road led down to the McCready's beautiful house where Mrs. McCready let me help her clean the bathrooms and make the beds, and where I would sometimes make believe I was working as a maid in a large and elegant hotel. Mr. McCready reminded us of Peter Rabbit and the little robin's "I implore you to exert yourself!" to Peter when the buttons of his little blue coat caught in the mesh fence in the garden. We thought no more of the fact that Mr. McCready was the manager of the Hanford nuclear plant that spilled radioactivity into the environment, contaminating the air, milk and water in ten counties and delivering intensive doses of radiation to babies and children, than if he had run the local fruit cannery. Only later, after we had moved to Wells, Nevada, where nuclear testing was then taking place in the southern desert, did we think much about the fact that we had lived so near a nuclear plant. This was a few years before people started putting bomb shelters in their backyards and signs identifying shelters were placed on public buildings. The nightmares I later had about radiation seeping under the doors and through the windows in spite of the blankets and newspapers we stuffed in every crack, included the sense that the greatest danger came from the invisible, the untouchable, and this seemed worse than "the Russians."

All the families who lived along our road had kids who belonged to the 4-H club. I raised a calf named Valentine, training her to halter lead and coaxing her in circles around the paddock for judging at the county fair. The judges tried to award everyone a prize and the only time I missed was when Valentine took a little nap in the dusty ring while my friends sauntered by, their calves' heads held high, hooves prancing through the dirt. We spent long afternoons playing house and horses and army, and made milkweed stew and mud pies laced with the blackberries that grew in dense bunches by the road. I hid in the tall weeds, mounted on my invisible but spirited palomino, narrowly escaping capture by my sheriff brother and the neighbor boys' posse. The road led to the cool mystery of dark raspberry bushes sheltering rabbits and snakes and possibly desperate tramps who would pull us into the bramble cave if we let our attention wander. I joined the Methodist Youth Fellowship, where I edged around the periphery of groups, helping out with the fairs, and going through the motions of Halloween parties, cakewalks and box socials. My mother tucked a lunch of fried chicken, pickles, apples and bread and butter sandwiches into a shoebox decorated with red construction paper for the Valentine's Day box lunch social, but I dreaded having it bid on, knowing I would have to eat with some boy I didn't know and who probably didn't even like bread and butter sandwiches. Just up the hill, our closest neighbors were Seventh Day Adventists, both alien and intriguing, who didn't work after sundown Friday and didn't eat meat. Another neighbor, my mother's friend Adelaide Burgess, though small and plain, carried an aura of deep mystery, her divorce shaping her as dark and secretive, someone you wouldn't want to know too much about. The fact that her children knew the pleasure of store-bought bread and dry cereal, however, very nearly compensated for her moral shortcomings.

On Heck Road my mother milked Ruby, our velvet Guernsey, grew lush gardens of corn, peas, beans, and a tangle of cucumbers and squash. It was only last summer, at age eighty-nine that she finally gave in to the unforgiving, nitrogen-dense garden she had been fighting since she moved to her last house. She claimed she was finally giving up gardening. Yet, now, wandering through her disconnected fragments of memory, she plans another garden, thinks about fertilizer and wheelbarrows and seedlings. She froze and canned vegetables, made pickles and jams and jellies and killed the chickens and rabbits for stews and frying. We screamed hysterically, with as much excitement as fear, when the beheaded chickens launched themselves wildly across the dirt yard and we carefully looked away from the rabbit pelts hanging inside the shed. She baked great loaves of bread, twisting the leftover dough into crusty, golden, fried bread sticks that we rolled in powdered sugar as she lifted them from the bubbling grease. Any time she had left to herself, she painted. Her self-portraits or still-lifes reflected what was readily available, eggplants, peppers, gourds and wild flowers. My father spent the days on the tractor or irrigating in the fields, home at night to dinner, coffee and his pipe.

When my father killed a deer on the only hunting trip he would ever take, it hung in the garage for a day, creating in us a squeamish excitement and the sick thrill of horror. A neighbor helped him clean and carve the deer, and mother wrapped it in tight white packages for the freezer. Mother served venison that winter, and dad pretended to be proud of himself for being the source of our food, but all of us were relieved when the deer was finally gone. We had done no better with the pig my parents had raised for food. That pig lived in a pen just behind our house and joined us at play, running up and down the fence, squealing and snorting, or prancing to greet us as we got off the school bus in the afternoons. We scratched him behind his ears and under his chin, his eyes closing in delight, snuffling pleasurably. The butcher came while we were at school one day and the pen was empty when we got home. We ate the pork chops and bacon with guilty obligation.

Like many farm families, all five of us children shared the same bedroom and none of us ever had our own room. We played games together, worked together and lived our lives together as children, separately from our parents whose problems or plans we thought little about. There were always enough of us for a game of *Authors* or *Old Maid, Parcheesi* or *Monopoly*. We ate whatever was served, wore the clothes my mother bought either at second-hand stores or through the J. C. Penney or Sears catalog, and accepted the lack of choice in those matters as we accepted the necessity of going to school, doing chores and doing homework. The feeling of being completely immersed in a family, part of something enveloping while not being ultimately responsible for anything, was comforting. The family was a given, living to its own rhythms, leaving each of us plenty of room to do our own dance. I could feel integrated, safe, incorporated and at the same have plenty of room to feel alone.

Johnny and Holly and I walked to school together, through a field of stubble and stones to a county road where we waited for the school bus. By the time we got there, my socks had bunched down into my shoes and the sandwich I carried for lunch had already seeped oily spots on the newspaper mother had wrapped it in. I held it away from my body to keep my blouse clean. I was convinced that the

discrepancy between my life as it was and the success and happiness I wanted was
to be found in not having a fried egg sandwich on homemade bread and apricots we
picked from the neighbor's tree for lunch, but instead a tuna fish sandwich with
iceberg lettuce on white, store-bought Wonder bread, wrapped in wax paper and
snuggled into a small paper sack with a crinkly package of potato chips and a big,
thick-skinned orange. It would have never occurred to my mother that not having
the right clothes or the right lunch bag was of any consequence.

Mother and Daddy were the powerful force in the background, giving our lives
shape, but we had no clear picture of who they were beyond being our parents—
there for us, doing not terribly interesting things that seemed to fill their days. Their
relationship with each other was equally obscure to me. I got some sense of their
relationship being real and complex when I went with my father to buy a Mother's
Day card. He thoughtfully selected one depicting a young woman wearing a black
sheath dress and a black felt hat with a real tiny feather secured by a spray of
sequins. It was a vision, an ethereal image of femininity totally at odds with the
mother we knew—garden soil trapped under her fingernails, hanging stiff laundry
on the clothesline in bitter cold, baking bread and frying chicken. Yet it was an
expression of how my father envisioned her and a vivid image of who we thought
she wanted to be.

My mother tells me she spent her childhood in one of Bonne Terre, Missouri's
"best families," and she assumes all of her children, brought up on the fringes of
poverty, carry with us the same sense of place and belongingness she brought with
her into adulthood, even as our own lives were shaped by living on the edges of
towns, while she had lived at their center. She grew up in the parsonage next door
to the Congregational church where her father preached. The acreage was fenced
in black wrought iron, and tall gates gave access to the house and tennis court.
Church Street ran in front, a quiet street leading to the library and other tidy brick
houses. The children played among the fruit trees, read the books they borrowed
from the library across the street, and swam every summer afternoon, all afternoon,
in the community pool. On school days they walked home for lunch, usually to
macaroni and cheese or Spanish rice. During the Depression my grandmother could
almost always make a good meal for her family and anyone else who dropped by
at suppertime if she had a can of tomatoes and a bag of rice.

My mother's mother sent her children outside to play as soon as breakfast was
over and expected them to entertain themselves until suppertime, much as her own
mother had done. That meant they rode bikes, went fishing, went to the library,
hiked in the woods, and generally did what they wanted as long as no one
complained about them. They either endured or enjoyed the little time they spent
with their parents, but for the most part they accepted them as normal, not very

interesting fixtures in their lives. They ignored their problems. My grandfather had several affairs when their five children were young, and my grandmother had what was referred to as a nervous breakdown. My mother's response to this was primarily irritation at her mother's tears and self-pity and an active effort to avoid being alone with her.

By the age of thirty my mother had five children. One photo on my desk shows her in our front yard in Carroll Acres, hand on hip, head cocked to the side, flared shorts revealing lean legs. There are other photos of her writing, keeping books, skimming milk. I now know, having had two children, that her daily life must have exhausted her. The admonition that a mother spend "quality time" with her children flourished in the post-war suburbs, where women were expected to develop their identity from their homes and families, but women on the farm, who had their hands full just keeping up with the work, were shielded from the Freudian wisdom that they could unconsciously relegate their daughters to years of frigidity or their sons to hell fires of homosexuality through a mothering misstep.

When my mother was fifteen, she left the small mining town where she had grown up and went to art school at Washington University in St. Louis. She first boarded with strangers who treated her like a servant, and finally went to live with Aunt Em, her Dad's sister, in what she calls a "cold water walk-up." While she had little money, what mattered to her was being able to go to school. Her father sent her $1.00 a week for shampoo and extras. She told me this story because I refused to go to the university if I couldn't afford to live in the dorm.

In all of our houses, my mother still lived part of her life in the airy upstairs studios of her art school, the air punctuated by the heavy scent of turpentine and linseed oil, and the powerful smell of the ochres and burnt siennas on her palette. She found us lunch money, wrote notes excusing our absences, returned the calls from our teachers, but these were things she *did*, not who she was. She seemed most real for us somehow when she was doing things that didn't include us, that outlined her for us as a completely separate person with a life unconnected to ours. Many afternoons we came home from school to find her standing at her easel, the mysterious vermillion and cobalt smudged fresh over the dried dark puckers on her wooden palette. She brought her studio, her friends and her fullness to our house on Heck Road, and we felt included in the romance of the past she pulled into the room. She seemed fully there when she sat at the kitchen table reading the paper, hair pushed behind her ears, her coffee cup breathing softly into her face. And when she was soaking in the bathtub, knees akimbo and belly breaking the water, the *New Yorker* pages already wavy from slipping into the tepid water, insisting that we leave her completely alone in the one bathroom in the house, all was well. When she was absorbed in something far from us, the safety and comfort we felt quietly anchored us to each other and to home.

She was a visitor in the houses where we lived. She cleaned and swept and washed the clothes, hanging them on the line. I remember the clean smell of cold sheets, the feel of rough towels frozen into stark figures, shapes we couldn't fold but clumsily maneuvered through the doorway into the house. They almost immediately became limp, losing their strength, and we rolled them into neat packages to iron later or spread them into tents on chairs and tables, floating over our secret games. She made pickles and apricot jam, baked bread and constructed soups of bones and vegetables from her garden, but even while she did this, her real life was in an art studio with men with names like Emerson Browning Barron and John Petro Tosco. There, her jeans and shirt were replaced by the knee-length wool skirts and sweaters and matching socks she wore with her saddle shoes. At other times, she was even younger, in the living room with her parents' friends, listening to Martin Eichenlaub play the piano, or sitting at the long tables in the library reading books the librarian had set aside for her. The choice she had made to marry my father brought her to the rooms we all occupied, but her time in them for all those years was temporary, an impermanent condition, rather than her life.

Later, I found myself resenting the fact that we never had the books she talked about as filling her summer afternoons and winter evenings, and that she never seemed bothered by the bleak emptiness of our cultural life in places like Wells, Nevada or Prosser, Washington as it contrasted with the richness of hers. It's taken a long time to realize that my mother didn't live that same bleakness even though she was in it with us. She was still fueled and nurtured by the abundance with which she had grown up.

We went to Bible school during the summers, which gave my mother a break from all of us, and which made me feel virtuous and useful, gluing little houses together out of Popsicle sticks and learning Bible verses. During the summer in the recreation program offered by the city, we learned to play tennis from a handsome and tanned husband and wife team, most memorable even then because they wore rubber thongs instead of tennis shoes. We swam in the public pool, and in the afternoons learned to make key chains and bracelets out of long, colored strands of plastic that we wove together in patterns. For one week each summer we went to church camp, packing a small suitcase and driving to the mountains with some other kids in one of the parents' cars. Mostly I remember how the shower room smelled and walking into the big dining hall alone, proud of my new cotton shorts and matching blouse. I faithfully tried to find Jesus in my heart, sitting alone, searching until I was in tears. After my parents had gone to all the trouble to send me, and the counselors had been so patient and helpful, it seemed wrong not to find Jesus before the week was over.

Poorly prepared to understand drinking as a problem, my mother easily and early saw herself as a victim of my father's drinking, a position from which she had difficulty regaining a sense of power. This was due, in part, to the limited choices she had with five children during the 1950s when her labors in the garden, the fields, with farm animals and chickens, were essential for the survival of the family. Her background hardly equipped her for the life she had with my father, living in ugly little houses in small towns, having few friends and almost no intellectual stimulation, seeing her life change in ways she had never anticipated, her talent and creativity draining from her while she struggled to keep the family well fed and clothed.

She sometimes felt split and disarrayed, disappointed in the life she had chosen, trapped by children and a lack of money, but this feeling was subterranean, pooling beneath the responsibilities she took for granted. She has never once intimated that she resented her children or longed for a different life than she had, even though it was far from the life she planned and from the one she would eventually find. However, she was blaming and resentful of my father and the restrictions brought to her by marriage, wanting and expecting more but not seeing her way clear to leave what she had chosen.

We, as children, did not experience her as angry, but as "other," not intimately connected with us, although at the same time she was the mainstay of our lives. If she was not there when we came home from school, the house felt dark, cold and unwelcoming, and as soon as she entered, it brightened and warmed with her presence. My sister and I complained loudly about the messes and disarray she left in her wake, undoing our hopeless efforts to transform the spare places we lived into the fairy tale living rooms we were beginning to see on television. Yet, we welcomed the safety and warmth she brought with her. Her own mother had shown little warmth to her children directly, but had cared for them well with a pleasant home, good meals, clean clothes, and the freedom to play and move freely in their world.

We were aware of tensions between my parents, but were disinterested in their problems—financial, emotional or otherwise. We didn't want to know their problems. We couldn't do a thing about them. Just as my mother had no sympathy for her mother's tears when her father was unfaithful, we didn't want to hear things about our father that diminished or demonized him, which is how we interpreted her complaints. Over the years, my mother's vision of my father's qualities narrowed to exclude almost any but those tied to his drinking, captured in the oft repeated description of the "long, lonely nights watching for his headlights to come down the road" and his other failures, both as a husband and as a father. Especially after his death, his children's view expanded to an appreciation of the most mundane and ordinary efforts he made as a father, taking us to church, buying ice cream cones, or waking us up in the morning with an irritating rhythmic "psssst" whispered from the doorway of our bedrooms.

We never lived anywhere you could call pretty, or even well cared for. Even when I was in college, my parents' home was functional; warm in winter, cool in summer, providing shelter and some comfort, but it was never inviting, not a place our mother identified with or that she saw as reflecting her at all. She just didn't notice the house; she loved the privacy and responsiveness of the garden and every summer afternoon found her crouched in the tomatoes or hoeing the rows of beans, focused and happy. Growing up in houses that were not homes, only places we temporarily stayed while on our way to someplace else, even if it was someplace just the same, gave me the strong desire to make a house a home. It stood for stability, and at the same time, it stood for independence and freedom. It gave me a sense of power and permanence. During times of enormous pressure or personal disarray, my floors go un-swept and dishes pile up. When I am gripped by hopelessness or worry, my house becomes shabby and dead. When I am taking good care of myself, the floors are vacuumed, the plants watered and the tables polished. I wonder if my mother's abandonment of her house reflects those feelings, or if she just liked the gardening better. For a while, I had a housekeeper every week, but I missed the connection I had with my house. When I didn't dust the paintings and move the furniture and polish the silver, they separated from me, became lifeless. Sweeping, or oiling the furniture, or smoothing the sheets over beds connects me with those things that I have chosen as reflections of me. The houses I raised my children in were reflections of my desire for a place of grace and beauty, more like the hotels we visited on our trips than the houses I had lived in. When I had little money, the gauzy curtains pulled back from the windows, the painted chests and chairs, the flowers on the sill, still communicated to me the value of my daughters and me as a family.

My parents lived together for twenty-five years, building a complex web of emotion, sex and responsibility that daily reflected the disparate backgrounds from which they came. We saw them as completely separate from us and almost one-dimensional. We were not clear on their personalities, their wants or needs. We knew little about their backgrounds other than what we saw when we traveled with them to visit family. Their relationship was not accessible to us any more than it was understandable to them. We took their presence in our lives for granted and built a world from which they were largely excluded. Our emotional lives were built around each other just as theirs were built around themselves. Mother was at one and the same time the most important presence in our childhood and yet, almost unknown to us. My father was important to us, but he didn't make the house a home. Like us, he lived there, he ate and slept, and came and went in his own world. Mother was home.

＊ ＊ ＊

We didn't live on Heck Road more than a few years, but those years became the center of the spoke around which the other towns, farms and cities were organized in my memory. It was on Heck Road that I first smelled the soft, musky smell of childhood sex, burrowed in the furrows of the pasture with a boy named Calvin while our parents drank coffee in the kitchen. We moved from small town to small town, my father trying to farm or otherwise support us, my mother feeling she had no choice but to go with him, unloading what little furniture and few clothes and dishes we had in one unwelcoming place after the next. We put newspapers on the shelves of the kitchen cupboards and mopped and scrubbed the scratched linoleum. We swept the cobwebs from under the eaves, cleaned the windows with vinegar and water and made the beds with thin sheets and my dad's old army blankets. We began anew. We moved every time my father lost a job or thought he had found one that would not shame him, leaving behind dark and hollow houses for new ones that were as cold and empty as those we had left. Salvation Army beds and dressers could be found in any town, and the few blankets and clothes and dishes we owned worthy of moving could be packed into boxes and follow us on a bus or truck. The furniture was stiff and naked, serving as a place to do homework or tell stories, not the polished wood and silk prints in my grandmother Stewart's living room. The houses we lived in mirrored the houses my father had grown up in where linoleum or bare floors, bed frames of curved pipe metal with loud springs and thin mattresses covered with one sheet and a wool blanket, rough and scratchy. What money there was went to the crops and equipment, and the house was a complete afterthought. It was not until my parents were on the edge of divorce in 1969 that they had a home that was other than purely functional, and that was after Johnny, Holly and I were in college or on our own and the younger boys were in high school.

We followed my father's attempts to make a living managing poultry farms and farming, later moving to be close to the territories he was responsible for as a conservation agent with the U.S. government. We lived on the social and physical outskirts of whatever town we were in. Whether we lived in Whitstran, or Bellingham or Prosser, Washington, we found names that described the places we lived, like "This Old House" or "The Prune Orchard." We were never in any of these places long enough to have any sense of being part of the community, which may be why I have no continuous memory of place, only snippets from here and there, glimpses of neighbors or schoolrooms, but nothing ongoing and solid. The communities seemed layered; families that belonged there, had deep, solid roots in ranches, farms or businesses, and the others, like us, who were passing through and would never have the history required for fitting in. Those omnipresent romantic images of small town warmth and acceptance are belied by the reality of rejection and insularity we experienced. There was a pretty clear line between "them" and "us." You could see it in the moms—their moms knew just what casseroles to bring and where to put them at the community center performances, or made the hamburgers and hotdogs we ate while watching the little league games, or were fixtures every afternoon at the drug store, hair cut sensibly short or tightly permed, eyebrows arched, darkened lips, outlined and severe, drinking Cokes and coffee and talking about high school teachers or bridge or recipes. In fact, the feeling of difference may have fared us well. We were misplaced, sidelined and often invisible, but we were moving on, not settling there and we were not burdened by the necessity of making a house or a town a home when it was only ours temporarily.

My mother has no recollection of being poor when we were growing up. All of her children do. She seemed to superimpose her own childhood onto the years that we had so little. She has often said that she resented living the way she did when we were growing up, but she means she hated my father's drinking and absence. I wonder at this discrepancy. What world was she living in? I remember using an outhouse, going to charity Christmas parties, shopping with my mother in second hand stores, seeing her cry when she learned I needed dental work. I began a life of quiet observation, going through the motions at school, sharing little, having few and sometimes no friends, and completely separating my life at home from that outside. I think all three of the older children in the family felt like outsiders, and that surprised my parents. The two younger boys were marginally integrated into the life of high school, but never expected to become the very successful attorneys they are today. On the other hand, my mother, who had never felt like an outsider, always had a secure and internal confidence that grew from a childhood in which she felt entitled. This confidence was nurtured by the many responsibilities of raising five children, cooking, gardening and making-do. When she says, "we might not have had any money, but we were never poor," she is talking about her experience during the years we were growing up, not ours. Well, at least not mine.

A child's needs were viewed as basic: food, shelter, parents and friends. No one paid a lot of attention to the process of growing up to make sure it was happening on time, and in the right direction. Life would unfold, you would grow up, life would go on, and you might as well not make a big fuss about it. To not stand out or be set apart was the surest avenue to freedom. Standing in line in a shopping center with my little sister and brothers, in scuffed brown oxford shoes, worn down on the outside, looming over the other children, waiting to see Santa Claus and feeling too old to be comfortable, I felt both embarrassed and responsible. I was obligated to tolerate what I was sure were the disdainful and disapproving comments and glances of others, and I endured these moments with the awareness that my role as a member of my family overshadowed the importance of whether I wanted to stand in line or not. There were some times, swinging alone on the playground at a new school, playing 7-Up with a big red rubber ball, looking down the aisles for someone to sit by on the school bus, finding a place to sit in the cafeteria, when I felt complete disconnection from anyone else, and extreme isolation. I felt this to be ordinary, and while I didn't have any expectation that it should be different, I didn't think it would last forever.

When I was fifteen, we moved to Wadsworth, Nevada, a tiny town about thirty miles east of Reno, almost abandoned now. The town had been a thriving railroad stop and switch station, but now was left with only a couple of bars, a dirt playing field, a combined store-post office-gas station, and one antique shop that also sold beautiful hand-made moccasins, beaded richly on soft deer skin. On the north, the town butted up against the Paiute Indian Reservation, thirty or so small wooden houses sitting in the middle of dirt patches scattered along two or three sandy paths. The Truckee River marked the other edge and beyond those boundaries was desert. Most of the families who lived in Wadsworth were Basque or Italian. Their families had ranches along the river that had been deeded to them over a hundred years earlier from Indian land. The Ceresolas, the Depolis, and the Echeverias formed the core of the town. There were a few Mexican families, the Gamboas being our closest neighbors. The twenty or so other families who lived there either worked on ranches, were back yard mechanics, or found some sort of work in nearby towns. The whites and the Indians were separated by a dusty road and were likely to come into contact only at school or at softball or basketball games, seldom socializing with one another. Both the Indian and white children from Wadsworth were bused to school in nearby Fernley, as were the Indian children from the reservation at Nixon. This reservation settlement was about thirty miles from Fernley, on the edge of the remnants of what had been Lake Winnemucca which had once covered all of the Great Basin. I started high school from Wadsworth, riding the bus with Indian girls whose families had known each other for decades, maybe even hundreds of years. The first few months they threw pieces of candy at me and made remarks about my hair or clothes, but by the end of the year, I had made friends with several of the girls in my class, although we never went to each other's houses. Mixing at school was acceptable, and some of the kids from Nixon were the most popular kids at school, but after school, we returned to our separate sides of the road.

During the summer of 1960, I was riding my horse, learning to shave my legs without gouging myself and planning the ways I would protect our house from nuclear fallout when the Russians bombed us. Life was largely built around school: drill team, games, dances, and friends. We spent afternoons reading movie magazines and a few decent books, my favorite being *To Kill a Mockingbird*. The bookmobile came to Wadsworth every two weeks and since we had usually finished the books days before, we couldn't wait to see it pull into the dusty empty lot by the post office. We talked about boys, and read books in which nurses and secretaries lived romantic, exciting lives, always struggling to maintain their sexual purity while being pursued by, then finally marrying, handsome, rich doctors and lawyers. The stories always ended happily—the goodness and innocence of the heroine winning the love of a decent but vulnerable man who was forever fighting off the advances and temptations of a sexually available, manipulative and seductive "other woman." Stories like these helped clarify the expectations for our futures and revealed our destiny in a simple and unambiguous way. These were simple stories of light vs. dark, good vs. bad, experience vs. innocence, and we knew exactly which side of the fence we wanted to be on.

The days blurred into one another, marked only once in a while by a trip to Reno or a visit from a friend. Following long sleepy mornings, the summer afternoons in that dusty town droned on seamlessly. I spent the early hours of the hot afternoons sitting on the floor of my room, which had been a sun porch, reading movie magazines and listening to the top forty on the radio. The town came to life around the little league games that started every other evening around six. Some of the mothers would make hamburgers and serve Cokes from a little trailer, and whether we were teenagers or four years old, housewives or ranchers, we were there. Nothing else was happening. Outside of the bookmobile and the little league games, the only activity was walking to the store for candy or ice cream, or riding bikes down back alleys and on the broken streets. Sometimes in the late afternoons, my parents would take us all to Pyramid Lake for a few hours of swimming and sunning, although it seemed perfectly pointless to my sister and me to go to the beach when it was too late in the day to get a suntan. My mother sat on the beach counting heads as she had always done, warning about sunburns, broken glass, drop offs and undertows. That is exactly what I did when I later took my own daughters to the lake or beach, and I now hear the familiar worries of my daughter as she cautions her own child against these timeless dangers.

While I was in college, my father homesteaded some property near Gerlach, a tiny town on the edge of Nevada's Black Rock Desert, about one hundred miles north of Reno. He wanted my mother to agree to live with him there in a trailer until he could build a house. His plan, the first step on his path to wealth, was to grow and sell sugar beets. He knew the land, having been over it many times in his capacity as a soil conservation agent, and he knew that with water close to the surface and a train running alongside the property, the investment would be lucrative. Mother refused to leave Reno, knowing she would be alone with my two younger brothers on a thousand acres of sand, no one to talk to, totally isolated from libraries, church, stores and other people. Having failed to get my mother to move to Gerlach, when he remarried after their divorce, he made a concerted effort to get his new wife to move to Gerlach but she dismissed the possibility without a moment's hesitation. He eventually sold the property and bought a run-down trailer park (C-Mor) on the outskirts of Reno, establishing the base to start the little empire he had been planning since he left the farm.

For several years, my brother, my dad, my mother and I were all at the university at the same time. My father went back to college to finish his undergraduate degree and then his Masters while I was in college. He built a simple desk between the closet and the window in the bedroom my three brothers shared. This plank desk, smelling of his pipe and work clothes, stacked with books and mimeographed assignments, separated him from us and made his life, which already was mostly spent away from us, even more distant and unknowable. After my father finished college, and about the time my parents were seriously talking about divorce, my mother returned to the university to get her teaching certificate. My parents were soon finished with each other and trying to put together plans for separate lives. My dad seemed less successful at first, moving into a cramped room with a hot plate and a cot in a dreary rooming house near the downtown casinos. We hesitated to visit my dad there. We thought it would embarrass him for us to see him in that place. A month later, he quietly moved into a much nicer apartment, deciding, I think, that two weeks was punishment enough. Within weeks he met and married his second wife.

Mother stayed in school and kept teaching. She did her work on the dining room table, facing the open kitchen door, available for our intrusions and questions and wants. She seemed perfectly comfortable writing papers and taking exams in classes with young people whose lives hadn't strayed, who hadn't seen the birth of five children, who hadn't picked grapes in Washington or flung beheaded chickens across a dirt yard.

II
If It Feels Good . . .

Calmly, and with a sense of great importance and some foreboding, I sat with the girls in my fifth grade class in 1955 and listened to lectures about menstruation and pregnancy, long before I had even the barest buds of breasts or any sense of myself as sexual. The sample box of Kotex and the Kotex belt all the girls received as a reward, supplies that were to pave our way to true womanhood, stayed hidden away in the back of my dresser drawer for years before the long awaited arrival of the first bloody spots. And these came none too soon—I was almost out the door to college before there was any assurance that I was, in fact, a real woman.

Menstruation was about the closest relative to sex I could imagine, except for the actual tampons I found in my mother's dresser drawer. These were casually tossed there with the girdle and stockings and they laid claim to her assured status as a woman, a woman who engaged in the dark mystery, more than did the fact that I woke every day with three brothers and a sister. Once in a while, my parents would exchange glances at breakfast, or my father would caress my mother in a certain way that embarrassed me for its intimacy, its suggestion of sex, but the distance between those early morning remnants and the secrets of their darkened bedroom was great. I walked by their open bedroom door one night on the way to the bathroom, hearing their unfamiliar words of passion, their voices pitched at a tone both desperate and ragged, and crept back to my room excited and disgusted by their animal sounds, confused the next morning when they drank their coffee and ate their oatmeal as if nothing had happened. I had fully anticipated, judging from all that noise and carrying on, that they would look different or make some announcement, something, after what had clearly been a life-altering moment, and was confused when they went on as usual the next day. My father never mentioned sex to me, but even while I was in college he would drive the thirty miles from Fernley to Reno, unexpectedly appearing at my apartment, and whether it was 6:30

in the morning or 10:00 at night, we both pretended he had just dropped by for a cup of coffee or to bring me something I needed, rather than to check on me and make sure I was behaving myself.

During my early high school years, at least in the isolated Nevada towns where I lived, being interested in boys was not the same as being interested in sex. Wearing a letter jacket or having a boyfriend was a high priority, but the actual possibility of having sex was still pretty far down the road. Not that my friends and I weren't hearing a lot about boys and their desires, how they couldn't control themselves if they were sexually aroused, how they just wanted sex and nothing more, but these warnings tended to make them seem foreign and unknowable, leading us to view them as unpredictable and weird rather than interesting or attractive. Attitudes about boys also separated girls from each other; the good girls, us, were normal, healthy and had sunny futures guaranteed as long as we "saved ourselves" for the right man. The others, the bad girls, who we were sure had deep character flaws proven also by their smoking and dyed hair, were doomed to a life of misery and social ostracism at worst, maybe a double-wide in the desert at best.

It is no surprise that young men and women easily became objects to one another. During the years of grade school and junior high in the 1950s, boys and girls were often split from one another, in school, on the bus, in the cafeteria and in after-school activities. Only during high school did we begin to make tentative steps toward one another, and the shadow of sex loomed so darkly over us that we could not clearly see one another as members of the same species. We learned to view boys through the lens of stereotype, as they did us. At school dances or on the few dates I had in high school, there was nothing to talk about, no common ground, and a great deal of attention was paid to avoiding sweating hands and not giving the "wrong signals." I heard a lot about "prick teases" and "guarding your virginity" long before I had any sexual interest in boys.

Would my grandmother White have preferred these awkward gropings and perspiration laced embraces to the afternoons she and Pop spent visiting over the fence that separated their farms near Sikeston, Missouri, or walking with him to the mailbox or church? Was she any less prepared for loosening the constraints on her body and her feelings than we were with our sure knowledge that boys only wanted one thing? For us, sex was what boys were after and what girls were taught to withhold, and we were devoted to keeping boys at arm's length while still allowing them a little enjoyment. We had a lot to lose; not just our virginity, which would be bad enough and mark us as unfit for marriage, but if we got pregnant our lives as girls were over. We would be catapulted into womanhood, with its weighty responsibilities and dreary, repetitive days of dishes and childcare. Giving into the potential momentary pleasure offered by another body was fraught with danger. It would result in a transformation of the self, both frightening and irrevocable. Only if we were married to him would the boy who "got us pregnant" be responsible for that transformation. And, even if sex didn't result in pregnancy, we were assured that "going all the way" was likely to result in us being tossed aside for someone not tainted by the loss of virginity.

During my late teenage years, sex was at the center of a quiet but physical battleground. I never went on a date during the first couple of years of college that didn't have the specter of sex and what to do about it shadowing the entire evening. From the minute a date called, foremost in the minds of most girls, even before what they would wear and how they would do their hair, was what to do about sex: how far to let him go, what to do if he tried something you didn't want like putting his hand on your leg in the movie, what to do if he wanted to hold your hand, or to kiss you. What about tongue?

Girls learned how important it was to protect a boy's ego even while resisting his sexual entreaties. His ego was inextricably linked with his penis, and our job was to find a way to keep him interested in us, not giving into sex while knowing what he really wanted was sex, resisting while not making him angry or hurting his ego. This was a pretty complicated assignment and the instructions were generally vague. This seemed a little easier for my grandmother Stewart, who said:

> *I went out with a fellow just when we first had cars, and we parked. I wouldn't spark. He took me home and started to try to kiss me and I hit him with my muff. If you spooned, he wouldn't have any respect for you.*

While women were considered the emotionally and physically tender sex, when it came to sex, men were the more fragile and delicate creatures. Not only did women need to be wary of hurting a man's ego through words or actions, thus damaging his sexual identity and performance, his sexual equipment was such that if he were aroused, he was not entirely responsible for his actions. Oddly enough, there was never a mention of the girl's ego, much less a suggestion that it would be important to consider it, nor, for that matter, was there much mention, if any, of the girl's sexual desires. Just as women couldn't forge a real identity until they found the right man, their sexual self was waiting patiently and quietly, almost inert, until awakened by a man's committed adoration.

 The idea of getting to know a boy was absurd; we just assumed he was manipulating and lying because that's what he thought he had to do, and he did, and we pretended not to know. We needed to keep him wanting us and he would only do that if we "held out." Oh, our parents, especially our dads, who spoke from their own experience, warned that he would promise otherwise, even say he loved us, and we expected him to say that, but neither girl nor boy believed it: it was something he needed to say to get past "first base." He resented having to be so dishonest and we didn't really want every boy who tried to maneuver us into sex to love us. We knew, however, that sex without the promise of love would brand us as loose or cheap. The message was clear: boys could not be trusted and even the nicest, most sincere boy could ignore you the next day at school if you finally gave in to him. They certainly weren't going to marry you, and they would have ruined you for anyone else.

While there might have been a sexual revolution recruiting women to become soldiers in service to men during the 1960s, sex was what men did to women, and whether women enjoyed it or not spoke more to their femininity than to men's lovemaking abilities. An erect penis demanded satisfaction. In translation, that meant to women that if they couldn't have an orgasm in the time a man required, particularly after he had devoted himself to a few thoughtful, perfunctory swipes at her clitoris or careless sucks on her nipples, it was just too bad. Besides, women weren't really expected to enjoy sex for the physical pleasure it gave us; we were to enjoy sex when we were loved by the man we would marry. It should please us to please our men.

It shouldn't be surprising that women who grew up in the 1950s and 1960s, focused on keeping themselves safe and pure, protecting themselves from men, saving themselves for the future, were not immediately sexually sophisticated and "in touch with their bodies" once relieved of that burden. These women who had grown up not acknowledging that they had autonomous sexual desires, who had learned that sex was always connected to a man, and, if it was good, connected to a man who loved you and who would marry you, were not likely to suddenly be intimately in touch with their own sexuality when they got married. In fact, it took years, decades, and many experiences for women of my generation to finally connect their sexuality with themselves rather than with someone else. The boys who had been brought up to see women as having something they needed for their own sexual pleasure also took a while to learn the importance of giving women pleasure, and this was a surprise for women who had assumed that men were the masters of sexual knowledge. Women who had learned that their sexual selves were to be awakened by a man who was the agent of action, one who "deflowered" them, who "took their virginity," assumed he would have some skill or innate ability in this matter. They were often surprised and disappointed to discover that his sexual talents were pretty limited and most likely to be self-serving. The romantic image girls grew up with, of the older, experienced, patient, generous lover, was pretty far removed from the guys they slept with who just wanted to have sex.

Small wonder that getting married was such an attractive goal. Not only would it prove the girl was normal and feminine, but it promised great relief from the lies and awkwardness of dating. In marriage, finally, after all the warnings about ruination, all the lectures about the devastating consequences of a misstep, women were expected to somehow enjoy sex. We would automatically become sensual, sexually alive, eager and responsive once we were a "Mrs." Once past this legal hurdle, if women didn't enjoy sex, they needed to work on their personality disorders, overcome their fear, their desire to dominate, or the masculine tendencies that led to their frigidity. Someone should investigate the forces that allowed generations of parents to convince their daughters that marriage vows would inexplicably change their bodies from their frozen, torpid state into wild, buoyant, welcoming pleasure centers. It is perhaps understandable that during the 1950s a small industry grew up around concerns about female frigidity—psychologists and scholars devoted themselves to unraveling this disorder that was not only hard on men's self-esteem, but in the guise of "refrigerator mothers," was likely to lead to autism, homosexuality, and other childhood disorders.

In the late 1950s and early 1960s, the cultural messages about sex were much more straightforward and universal than they were to become only a few years later. Television, novels, parents, teachers and other girls provided messages of over-whelming consistency and communicated the obvious as well as subtle distinctions girls had to worry about in order to remain valuable. "No petting below the waist" was a general rule, for example, modified incrementally by the length of time the girl knew the boy. Boys were easily aroused and since the consequences for girls were so serious we became sexual sentinels. The awareness that a man had an erection merged cold panic with a wonderful sense of power. On a date as a young woman I would be riddled with guilt at my unknowing ability to rouse a boy to a painful state, and was petrified that he would not be able to contain himself if he got too stimulated. Such constant vigilance dampened any incipient sexual stirrings and deflected any thought of actually enjoying the moment. Each interaction was a potentially embarrassing dance of physical expression and constraint, giving and withholding, and watchful, careful attentiveness.

One winter evening during my first year at university, a man I saw as far more experienced and mature than I took me to dinner at a Basque restaurant about an hour's drive out of town. After a meal more memorable for its size than its taste—which generally characterizes Basque food in Nevada, as well as several of the traditional and potent local Picon punches—we made our rather drunken way back to my dorm. During this trip, with one hand on the wheel, his other gently and patiently slid from the top of my thigh to my crotch, pulling my panties away, softly manipulating me. Desire was out of the question. I was instead tallying the tab for the evening: he'd paid for dinner, done all the driving, so clearly he could expect something, but what? Kissing? Tongue? Breasts? Or was I to touch him? Inside or outside his pants? The potential for pleasure from his touch was erased by these calculations. Intercourse? Not even a possibility. The geographical terrain between that and even the most heavy petting was wide and strewn with land mines.

Clearly, despite all the risks, a lot of girls in high school were having sex or we wouldn't have seen so many of our classmates take the bus or train out of town for a long visit with their "auntie" . . . but, every girl walking the hallways of her school could easily identify the "good girls" and the "sluts" and so could every boy. Losing our virginity, this "giving up" was a major transformation of identity. There was no going back. As I walked through the main entrance to my campus the day after I had sex for the first time, I knew everyone walking my way could sense the radical upheaval I had experienced, could see that I was born anew, ready to share secrets with other sisters in my new tribe.

For me and for my friends living in the dorm at the University of Nevada, having come from every small town in the state, and having every intention of getting our degrees in nursing or education and returning to those same small towns, our perception of identity rested heavily on who we were going to be with and eventually marry. Girls' awareness of the meaning of "losing their virginity" must have been a pretty heavy burden for some young guy who just wanted simple sexual pleasure. The young women I knew did not approach this first "change of life" casually. Until the passage of *Roe v. Wade* in 1973, and with our reputations always on the line, the withholding and denial characteristic of girls was just as predictable as the wheedling of boys. Not surprisingly, this contorted construction of sex and sensuality was a pretty poor precursor to deep sexual intimacy.

The sixties and seventies weren't only about sex, but they were very much about sex. While sex was joined with love and fraught with tedious conflicts in the 1950s, by the late-1960s sex was supposed to be uncomplicated and unlimited. We were supposed to be comfortable with ourselves, our sexuality, and to have long abandoned any expectation that there was a solid relationship between sex and intimacy, sex and love, or sex and the future. Sex was fun and sex was now. That was the ideology, but the reality was that the substantial imprint of the 1950s weighed down our sexual choices. Freedom was tempered with a good deal of bewilderment. After all the years of learning how to protect ourselves from men who "only wanted one thing," and after learning if we gave up our great prize, our virginity, we would be damaged goods, we were suddenly expected to throw ourselves into sexual relationships that were just for fun, to see sex as a harmless, natural way of spending the evening. The messages of the sexual revolution not only contrasted glaringly with what we had learned growing up in the 1950s about sex and its relationship to our future, the messages of the revolution were themselves convoluted. Underneath the apparent dramatic changes, the definitions of relationships remained pretty much the same.

The boys had a pretty sweet deal, which should come as no surprise since the sexual revolution really was an *accoutrement* to the male-led civil rights movement and anti-war movement. The insistence of the women's movement—that women had the same sexual rights as men—converged nicely with men's dreams of women as sexually available and uninhibited. Here were all these brave men, fearful of being drafted, worrying about going to Canada, fighting the war at home or working for freedom, and they had sexual needs. More recently, this sentiment reemerged, materializing as groups of women encouraging "giving it up" for the boys going to Iraq and Afghanistan. Long into the 1960s, we were still largely running the ditto machines and making the coffee, and we were either popular or wallflowers based on our desirability to men, just as we had been in high school. But with the sexual revolution, good, caring, loving women had sex with men, didn't withhold, and didn't "save" themselves. Women who had graduated from high school with a pretty long list of "do's" and "don'ts" were now to throw those rules aside and learn an entirely new game, a game with very few "don'ts."

Having learned about sex from the rulebook of the fifties, when the old rules were juxtaposed with the new, there was real confusion about the relationship between one's morals, one's body, and one's future. The contradictions couldn't have been made more clear to me than by my experience with our old family doctor. When Kelsie—whom I later married—and I began having sex, I decided to use the newly available birth control pills rather than to live with the specter of pregnancy hanging over my head. I approached Dr. Kernan with great trepidation to ask for a prescription. As I sat on the examining table in his office, wrapped loosely in a stiff, white paper gown, he kindly refused, admonishing me to pay attention to my studies and to worry about sex after I was married. Red-faced and ashamed, I slid awkwardly from the table into my clothes and finally, home.

Despite the vague feelings that there might be a price to pay for the freedoms women were enjoying, we were also eager to embrace these new freedoms, and were soon able to gather enough sexual experience to learn that sexuality was ours, not men's, that we were not simply passively awaiting being awakened by men. We had always been responsible for withholding sex, but now we had the choice and responsibility of deciding when to have sex and when not to, based on our own desires and assessments of risk. The lines that had been so clearly drawn became fuzzy. Marriage was seen as an outmoded holdover from the 1950s, and the wives who were our mothers were almost as guilty of maintaining the capitalist war machine as were the "organization men," so saving ourselves for marriage was no longer the ultimate goal. The old rules that had provided the boundaries for so many years didn't apply to the new game that defined marriage as the end of freedom, not just for men but for women.

Marriage was the symbol of stability, maturity, and the end of youth, and while we may still have held on to the core belief that marriage was our future, it was disengaged from our sexual identities, our sexual selves. Now, women who wouldn't sleep with a man before marriage could be painted as sexually repressed, uptight, uncool, frigid, and maybe even lesbian. Not wanting to be accused of any of these signs of a lack of femininity, not a few of us slept with guys whose names we didn't even know, guys we had never had a three minute conversation with, guys who didn't recognize us or acknowledge us the next day. Having sex was simpler, and often more comfortable, than having a conversation. There was no acceptable reason to not have sex in a culture of "if it feels good, do it."

Not only was sex divorced from marriage, sex for girls was often separated from the self. Modern girls were to disengage from their sexuality just as guys were to still see theirs as central to their masculinity. While before, girls were to hold on to their virginity as a treasured object, now girls were encouraged to offer them-selves sexually with little expectation that their sexuality had anything to do with their identity. Sex was still something girls could withhold or give up, but the emphasis was now on *giving* it rather than withholding. Their identity wasn't to be wrapped around their sexuality. The change was that the expectations for giving were different now that women did not secure their identity through surrendering their virginity to their husbands. Despite the nagging doubts that men might talk the new talk but walk the old walk and still want to marry a virgin, we pressed ahead with new sexual "freedoms."

Girls probably didn't learn about their own sexuality or their own bodies and begin to "own their sexuality" rather than see it as something they gave or withheld, until the women's movement became temporarily nearly obsessed with the types and gradations of orgasms women could have. Probably not until women's consciousness-raising groups began showing women how to give themselves gynecological exams, demonstrating the intricacies of their labial folds and calibrating their responses to different forms of stimulation, did women begin to take their own sexuality seriously as an integral part of themselves, rather than something they would hand over to someone, give away or bestow.

Although not every woman of my grandmothers' generation was as sheltered as mine, the vast majority were very protective of their virginity, and pretty quick to impose their rules on others. My grandmother Stewart said,

> *My friend Bea was kind of loose and we girls called on her and said if she didn't straighten up we wouldn't have anything to do with her. And she straightened up.*

Not only did my grandmothers not expect to have sex before they got married, their assumption was that no man worthy of their commitment would put them in that untenable position. As Inez Stewart told me,

*I would never have married your grandfather if he wanted to go to bed with me
before we got married. I wouldn't have had any respect for him.*

Her own daughter, my mother Helen, was not nearly as clear about that, and joined
many women of her generation who slept with their men before they went off to war
and certainly before they got married.

My grandmothers knew that their husbands would expect to have sex with
them, and they met that expectation, for the most part, with anticipation, and not a
little resignation. At the same time, they were both vaguely unsatisfied, figuring that
something their husband apparently enjoyed so much must have more to recommend it than they were getting. Like many women of their generation and circumstances—nice women, good women—they didn't expect to be thrown into wild
paroxysms of pleasure, but they seemed to carry a disappointment about what might
have or could have been. "I think women are so much slower, and often daddy was
through before I got started" was a complaint my grandmother Inez expressed that
didn't end with her generation, or her daughter's, or mine for that matter. Yet, their
experience was so limited that even if they had a vague sense that there was more,
they could not be sure, wouldn't have known how to ask, and would definitely not
have dreamed of searching outside their marriage for a more satisfying relationship.

My grandmother Stewart loved my grandfather deeply, but sex was definitely
for his pleasure rather than her own, and she thought my grandfather represented
most men. She even understood my grandfather's affairs at some level, saying:

*He needed more than I could give him. Sex was a little game men liked to play.
I knew it was expected if you got married, but it wasn't something you thought
you would enjoy that much. It was more of a duty because he wanted it. But you
had to be a virgin when you got married.*

One of the reasons my grandmother Stewart, like millions of women of her
generation, never fully enjoyed sex, was because she had no control over contraception and "was always afraid of having a baby, since you never knew which
time it would happen, and every time I was just nervous until that time of month."
Although during the later years of their marriage, after menopause, she began to
enjoy sex more than when she was younger, it was still not overwhelmingly
satisfying. From her perspective, sex was something men needed and women had
to provide, but the woman's sexual response was completely up to her. Foreplay,
a pretty troublesome concept in itself since it redefines much of what is most
pleasurable to women as secondary to the "main event," was often pretty
perfunctory, when it occurred at all. Women were to be available for their husbands' needs, but their own sexual pleasures were derivative or reflective, and for
my grandmother, something she might experience accidentally. Whether she had an
orgasm or not was up to her, reflecting her ability to "achieve" an orgasm, rather
than his lovemaking abilities. Not that my grandfather wasn't a loving man, a good

husband and a gentle man. But he was a man of his generation whose definition of sex and sexuality was built around men's needs and women's acquiescence. Two generations later, lying with the man who was to be my husband on his narrow bed, light playing on our bodies, I could have been my grandmother; he was someone I wanted to love me; he needed sex; and, whether I felt anything remotely like an orgasm was completely up to me, my body's response being something my body did, separate from me, not something we did through intimate caring and caresses.

My grandmother Stewart wove her sexual relationship with my grandfather into her marriage to him, and it was as much a responsibility as was shopping for groceries at Kroger's or making dinner. Her identity as mother, as wife, wasn't one that comfortably merged with a definition of herself as sexual. Women were as likely as men to divide women into categories, the kind of women men desired sexually and the women they needed to raise their children and keep their homes. Had she been given the choice, my grandmother would never have chosen sexuality over marriage, orgasms over commitment.

My grandmother White's sexual life was even less satisfying, but the emptiness she felt was saturated with the deep pain of never having been loved. Nor did she love my grandfather, although at first she liked and respected him. Sex for her was an unhappy obligation she met with resistance and resignation, laced with sadness.

> *I think most men are ready all the time. He was. I run from him lots of times. He said I was the iciest person he ever saw, but I just couldn't stand it so much. Once in a while, but every day I couldn't stand.*

Her sadness was more about lacking love than from lacking sexual pleasure, a longing for closeness she had craved since childhood. She had never been cuddled or loved or held as a toddler, and throughout childhood, when she should have been cuddled and cared for herself, she was instead caring for other children. She longed for the wholeness of an intimate connection. Her emotional generosity was clear to her grandchildren who gravitated to her warm, strong presence, but the relationship between my grandparents was characterized by duty and necessity rather than warmth or emotional generosity. Very simply, love and sex were powerfully connected for her, and the lack of love made sex with my grandfather unpalatable.

> *It wasn't anything like love. If he had loved me, he would have trusted me, but he never did. I saw it as a duty. When I got married, I knew that was one thing a man would want to do if he lived with a woman. At first, there were times I enjoyed it some. But mostly, I just knew it was something men had to have. Seems like that's how he saw it too. Like something he needed to do.*

While my grandmothers didn't think of sex as something *they* wanted, but rather as something men wanted, I believe the messages received by girls of my generation, at least middle-class or working-class girls, was much the same. One difference was that my grandmothers were not expected to agree to have sex before marriage nor were they expected to really enjoy sex after marriage. Unlike my grandmothers, we were expected to enjoy sex, but the enjoyment was a passive acceptance, a pleasurable giving rather than a lustful demand. My daughters' generation expects to enjoy sex and they seem to make decisions about their sexuality within a context of self-awareness. At the same time, the disembodiment of sexuality continues in the portrayals of sex as something that is done *to* one another rather than *with* one another within a framework of intimate connection.

Not talking about sex was the generally accepted rule through four generations of women in my family. To talk about "liking a boy" or "being in love" was okay, but "sex" was hidden under many levels of words that had nothing to do with organs or orgasms. Like almost every woman I know who grew up in the 1950s in this country, my mother never talked to me about sex, which was probably just as well. Friends who had that conversation reported that it left them embarrassed, sweaty and slightly incredulous. My mother's mother was spared the need to talk to my mom and her younger sister about sex because their older sister, Frances, was eagerly forthcoming, enrapturing the neighborhood children with lust-filled serial romances, explicitly describing steamy, wild sex. My mother was more likely to be found fishing or climbing the fences around the parsonage than listening to these racy romances. My grandmother would have been ill-prepared for such a venture in any case. She, like many women of her generation, had placed sex in the category of something to exchange for the love and commitment she wanted from my grandfather.

In 1942, my grandmother, Inez Stewart, offered some cautious advice about decorum to my nineteen-year-old mother when she took the train from Missouri to Texas to pin the wings on a boyfriend who was graduating from flight school. My mother still remembers that she wore a pillbox hat with a dove gray suit and white silk blouse and had lunch with her young man at the St. Anthony Hotel. Her mother never asked questions about her relationship or suggested that sex was a possibility deserving of mention, but only warned that she shouldn't discuss the trip with others when she returned. Nineteen years old, a long train trip, alone with the boyfriend who had been penned up in the barracks for months, and no words of caution, advice or wisdom. Surely the topic was not far from either woman's mind, but to bring it up was to acknowledge its possibility, which was not only uncomfortable, but shameful.

My oldest daughter, Tyler, would say that I never talked to her about sex; that it was hidden and secret, maybe even dirty. I could talk comfortably with my daughters about their bodies, their breasts, their periods, and could love and stroke their beautiful faces. But it was no easier for me to talk about them actually having sex than it was for my mother to talk to me about it, even though by all rights I should have overcome the sexual denial I had grown up with and embraced the new freedoms offered by the women's movement. We could talk about boys they liked, or cared about, but I saw the boys through my pre-sexual revolution eyes. I didn't want my daughters to be "used" or "hurt" which reveals the little faith I had in the sexual revolution changing the way boys and men thought about sex. And no wonder. My first husband never really "forgave" me for not being a virgin when we married in 1966, even though we too had slept together soon after we met, the first time in a cold spare bedroom of his stepfather's house where he had the foresight to stow a condom under the mattress. And my father, although my mother was otherwise faithful for thirty years of marriage, could never forgive my mother's sexual affair with someone she worked with in the civil rights movement. He was punishing and rejecting of her until the end of their marriage, and carried a deep bitterness toward her until he died, an attitude far more damaging and hurtful to him than to her. She never regretted the affair, although it holds no interest to her now, and saw it as helping her finally decide to leave a marriage in which she felt stifled and unreal.

My daughters' sexual freedom was not my foremost concern when I thought about them having sex. I worried about them getting pregnant, or getting AIDS or gonorrhea, and they probably learned from me more about protecting themselves physically and emotionally than about giving or loving or enjoying their bodies. My father's voice propelled me while my mother's embrace of the freedom of the "if it feels good, do it" ideology, which she shared with me after I was already divorced, ended with me, not translating into the messages I gave my daughters about sex. By the time I was ready to talk to my youngest daughter, Kate, about sex, having been made well aware of my inadequacies in that area by Tyler, I was willing to make a good stab at a very open, positive talk about sex being wonderful and hers to enjoy and about knowing her body and taking care of it. She absolutely refused to talk about sex with me. Wasn't interested, couldn't be bothered. That was then of course, and her attitude changed pretty dramatically, but she never did want to talk about sex with me.

All of the sexual relationships I had during the sixties and seventies had never translated into a feeling that my sexuality was my own. I had never been sexual for myself. Rather, having sex was a way to get closer to a man, or to accommodate him, his desires, his needs, or even to comfort him. The messages of the 1950s, which weren't very different from those of the 1920s, were firmly embedded in my personal rulebook. I hadn't found much of myself in those sexual encounters. Making love had eluded me during all those years of having sex freely and frequently. Many of us spent our young adulthood, and often our early married years, struggling to connect our sexual feelings with our core identity, to see sex as ours rather than something we did for someone else.

Often, in our forties and fifties, we begin to experience a full and lush sexuality, one less complicated and more integrated into our selves, yet one that contrasts dramatically with the public image of women our age. It seems almost a cruel joke that just as we finally begin to appreciate our sexuality and begin to have some confidence in our sexual selves, our sexual attractiveness to others is fading. Just when we could have robust, connected sex, we are being neutered by our culture and have to fight to keep any semblance of our sexual identity alive. Advertising, magazines, and film present young women, often girls not old enough to legally smoke or drink, as sexually desirable icons, their boyish bodies, firm breasts, flat stomachs, pouting lips signaling sexual availability and interest. In fact, these girls, if they have lovers who are anywhere near their own age, are likely to have lovers who are sexually inexperienced, selfish and not terribly adept at satisfying their partner and anyone older would probably be guilty of statutory rape. By the time a woman has had numerous lovers or husbands and/or a few children, she has learned about her own body—what positions allow her the most pleasure, how much pressure she likes on her nipples or clitoris, how hard or gently she likes to be kissed and made love to—she has a sexual depth and power that allow her to receive and to give great pleasure. Yet, by this time she is also facing a devaluation of her worth, a sense of shame or self-consciousness about her no-longer firm body. And if she is not married, she lives in a social world in which her sexual desirability is diminished, her visibility as a sexual being hovering near zero. She's likely, if she's anything like me, to experience a weird yo-yoing between desiring a sexual partner, seeing herself as sexual and desirable, at least to someone, and the bleak sense that she's past all that and needs to start devoting herself to horticulture or bird watching.

Kelsie, my first husband, and I planned to spend our honeymoon driving from Reno to Philadelphia where I was going to graduate school and he would find something to supplement my meager grant. On our wedding night we stayed in the bridal suite at the Continental Lodge in Reno, so designated, I imagine, because it was dominated by a king size bed. We had driven there after the wedding at my parents' house, exchanging uncomfortable conversational tidbits, frozen to the seats with the chill realization of the monumental change we had both just agreed to. I felt unreal, having gone through a ceremony which was to transform me from girl to married woman, but feeling instead the awkwardness and embarrassment of a junior high school girl at a dance in the school gymnasium. It must have been late, or we must have assumed we were supposed to go to bed and have sex, because we went from the car to the bed with little discussion or distraction. I changed my clothes in the bathroom, put on a filmy pink "waltz-length" gown, actually more "knee-length" on me because I am so tall, and slid awkwardly into bed where Kelsie awaited me silently, still in his underwear. I can only imagine that we had sex that night since it was an obligatory part of the wedding day, but I have no recollection of it.

I was taking a shower in a motel in Memphis, Tennessee when the emptiness I had chosen engulfed me. I missed my family, my school, my friends, and I missed the man who had been my first lover. Kelsie and I were already set on a road of togetherness characterized by grim obligation, an expectation about marriage I had learned well watching my parents. He seemed comfortable with that as well, that being what he knew, and our sexual intimacy was not so much intimate as it was compulsory during the years we were married. I was, like my grandmother, vaguely disappointed at the aridness of our sexual relationship, but by the same token, I didn't have great expectations. Sex was "performed" with little trust or openness, almost no sharing of feelings or appreciation of the other's body, just mechanical, usually unsatisfying plain old missionary style sex. We were never swept away by passion, never eager and aggressive with one another, never initiated sexual intimacy outside of bed. In bed, he lay on top of me, aroused enough for penetration, thrust into me, and after enough stealthy glances at me to realize I was going nowhere, he had an orgasm and slipped out of me. While he was still inside me, I could feel the incipient flutter of what I suspected might be an orgasm and I clung to that for a moment before letting go of him. I had read enough about romance and true love to dream of the marvelous magic of the merger of overwhelming love and fantastic sex, and was sorely disappointed by this pale imitation.

And, all the romance novels were right about sex with a man you loved being delicious and consuming and life affirming. But there is an undeniable time warp. This knowledge could not have been discovered by a scared and self-conscious twenty-year-old girl, who had never felt the inside of her body, never caressed her own nipples. This couldn't have been known by a girl who was fearful of being used and left, by being taken from, and who was therefore protective of herself. This couldn't have been known by a woman who had to give up her identity, or her work, to have the love and support of a man. It couldn't have been known with a man who couldn't love, or who could only see a woman as the necessary other, the presence required for his sexual satisfaction. It could only have been found when there was a man whose beautifully imperfect body mirrored my own, whose concerns and doubts were incorporated into a humorous and loving and warm person who had years to learn about himself, about children, about failure and desire and women, and who was strong enough and safe enough to love and give and want. It could come with safety and risk-taking and vulnerability rather than holding back or holding on to what I had for fear that once released or revealed it was gone. And it could only come after all the years of self-doubt and struggle for independence and identity led to a more comfortably imperfect and self-accepting person. And even though this love, this open sexuality with this man was somehow lost, the depth and richness gained from it remains.

During the years after Kelsie and I were divorced, having sex with the men I dated was no more meaningful than having a beer together or kissing them goodnight. The new sexual rules left little room for wavering or unwillingness. Men, unless they were clearly in the "friend" category, were available and expectant sexual partners. This was, mind you, before the "friends with privileges" relationships now accepted as ordinary. A picnic at the lake with a first date was followed by sex. When my date came in for coffee after a movie or dinner, we both expected to end up in bed. Sex accompanied almost any activity, as dessert followed the meal. Sex was separate from the expectation of love or commitment or marriage. Sex no longer intimated building a life together or having children together. Sex was not tied to dreams of everlasting love or white picket fences or really even caring about another person. Sex was sex; narrow, limited, and supposedly physically enjoyable. Young women, who no longer were saving themselves for marriage and who had finally been convinced that their virginity was not a gift they were to hand their groom on their wedding night, now saw sex as one of the ways in which they could fill the time with a date. Perhaps some of us also realized that even if the sex wasn't that good or exciting to us, men wanted it, just as we had always known they did, and there was no longer any reason to deprive them. It was not a big sacrifice for most of us, we didn't see having sex as morally corrupting us, and there was simply no reason not to. Having sex didn't bind us to anyone, didn't mean we had to commit ourselves to anyone, and it was easier to do it than to spend a lot of energy thinking or talking about whether we should or shouldn't or what it might mean. "Just do it" seemed the easiest response.

It may have looked like women were simply following the male model of sexuality that became commonplace later, disconnecting feeling from doing, seeing sex as a need. But looks are deceiving. Our patterns may have been similar, but their meanings were very different. Men incorporated sex as a natural part of who they were and defined it as something to attain. Women still viewed it as something they were giving, but not giving out of love or hope, but because there was no reason not to. No longer something to be saved, some valuable commodity, it was worthless, and should be made available upon request. It didn't define us, make us "good" or "desirable." It was ours to give or keep, but keeping it made no sense when giving it wasn't valued. That is, it had no currency. Despite all the talk about sexual freedom, women still weren't viewed as loving sex, wanting it, hot for it.

Those women, women who were sexual predators, were still separate from the rest of us.

Even though women of my generation in my situation were having sex easily and often, our response to our own sexuality was as diminished and disconnected as it had ever been. We had been raised to view ourselves as non-sexual, passionless women. The advertisements in the magazines our mothers bought or that we read on the newsstands showed young women together in fluffy peignoirs and "baby doll" pajamas, having tea together in their bedrooms, tiny fluffy dogs at their feet. They were bland and pure and innocent. The bed draped in a pure white spread could have been an altar on which they delivered themselves as gifts. Nothing in the picture hinted at passion, at lust, at animal urges, at hunger or desire or sweat or other juices; there was no moaning, no longing, no pulling and tearing at one another, no struggle. It was not until the 1970s that *Vogue* and other magazines showed women as sexually voracious, as lusting after men, longing for sex, wanting *it* rather than love. But the culturally approved relationship between women and sex was still an uneasy one. Women might have wanted sex, but there were heavy penalties and they had nothing to do with getting pregnant and having to marry the boy next door. Sex was dangerous. Men wanted sex, and were determined to have it and when women put themselves in a man's world, they put themselves in harm's way. The consequences were assault, rape and, sometimes, death.

Women's opportunities for sexual pleasure have grown with the generations, as have the openness about sexuality and a front and center attitude about sex expressed in the media. Innuendo and double entendre have given way to sexual display and open sexual banter on television, and to lyrics that are sexually explicit and often sexually violent. The treatment of sex is so blatant, so base, so frank and so graphic that children clearly don't get the same messages we did growing up, messages that reinforced the idea that sex was prohibited before, but sacred within, marriage. Yet, there is nothing in the portrayal of sex on MTV or HBO or in the games and media depictions that defines sex as more intimate than did those messages from the fifties. If sex was hidden and dirty, the explicit display of sex has done nothing to make it more natural or beautiful. Rather, it is presented as exploitative, aggressive or predatory for the most part, not part of a close and loving intimate relationship. Lovemaking has become fucking, and while it may be true that there is more fucking for both men and women, the kind of closeness and warmth and sexual expression that my grandmothers never found is not all that easy to come by a hundred years later.

Today, it seems to me, both men and women "have sexual needs," and each is free to use the other for their satisfaction, which is different from the experience of my generation of women who were really using sex as a means to please a man or to gain intimacy. But for my daughters' generation, the freedom to define themselves as sexual has not resulted in a redefinition of that sexuality to include easy, natural intimacy and warmth. It has instead resulted in the male definition of sexuality being impressed upon women. Sex outside of marriage is often as exploitative as ever, the difference being its generalization to include women's desires. The desire by women to merge sex and intimacy has not been fulfilled by this new acceptance of sex as just another animal need.

My mother saw her life as a series of stages; having sex was tied to the marriage stage. She didn't "save herself" for marriage, and her friends weren't all virgins when they got married; Fannie Snow, who dated my father before my mother did, sported six fraternity pins on the inside of her jacket lapel and it was assumed she had sex with each of the men who gave them to her. But for my mother, sex and marriage and babies were inextricably linked, inescapably and happily linked, and she waited for a time when all of those seemed possible with the same man.

The dramatic shift in the sexual lives of middle-class women from my grandmothers' and mother's generations during which sex—and not necessarily good sex—within marriage was the standard, to one in which sex and marriage were disconnected but in which both men and women expected to have fulfilling sexual relationships, is only visible from the vantage point of time, but its cumulative impact is great. My sexual identity and sexual opportunities seem to exist in a separate world from those of my grandmothers. At my age, their sexual identity was inseparable from their status of wife, and their sexual expectations were limited to fulfilling what they defined as the needs of their husbands. The restrictions on their sexual lives were strong. While my generation struggled a great deal with our sexual identity, and obviously did not completely reconcile the heavy messages of the 1950s with the equally heavy but contradictory messages of the 1960s, we incorporated a fuller, freer, less dependent sexual identity than did our grandmothers or mothers. The time we had to distance ourselves from the early confusing messages about our sexuality, messages that sex was dirty and bad outside of marriage and a pure and marvelous gift within marriage, was time well spent. By the time we had learned about our sexuality, we had also learned a great deal about ourselves.

My daughters and most of their friends are not as cavalier about sex as I was at their age, although they are no longer as constrained by worry about pregnancy and its consequences. They take the availability of birth control absolutely for granted, at least as I write this. That doesn't mean they take it lightly, but their decisions are of an entirely different nature than were ours or our mothers'. My mother's older brother and sister both married because of pregnancy and my mother's restraint was based in part on watching her brother's tears at the kitchen table when the parents of the girl he got pregnant came to have a talk with my grandparents and to make the unavoidable plans for marriage. My grandparents were deeply shamed and grieved by the obligatory marriage, but considered nothing else. These seventeen year old kids got married and lived unhappily together for a few years, before my aunt drove into a concrete embankment on the way home from a shopping trip. Years later, in the 1960s, not much had changed for the working-class couples written about by Lillian Rubin in her book, *Worlds of Pain*. She showed that these couples, who were desperate for a life better than that of their parents and different from the bleak obligations and narrow constraints they had grown up with, dreamt of escape from the limits of their blue-collar world. They had sex until they "got caught" and then they got married, becoming parents before they knew anything about loving one another or, for that matter, about themselves.

Sexual freedom is inseparable from the other freedoms women have gained. Women who either can or must support themselves are certainly less likely to tolerate sexual experiences that are as unsatisfying as those my grandmothers had. The "sexual revolution" was part of an increasing participation of women in every facet of society and would have meant little had it not been accompanied by the economic independence women have gained. Women who can support themselves, women who don't rely on men for the economic support of their children, are in a position to choose a partner for the personal, sexual and emotional gifts he can bring to a relationship, not the economic rewards he can offer, and they are likely to remain or leave for the same reasons. When a woman is free to choose a partner absent any economic consideration, her choice tends to be toward a loving, warm, giving, responsive man rather than one whose personal characteristics are overcome by what he has in his wallet. What he has in his pants still matters, but in an entirely different way.

III
May I Have this Dance?

My parents fell in love on a dance floor in Sikeston, Missouri during World War II, and like hundreds of thousands of young couples, they rushed to get married before my father was sent overseas. He never went overseas as it turned out, although my mother followed him from St. Louis to San Diego and a couple of places in between, riding the train with other young wives and soldiers, first as a bride, then as a young mother. A photograph taken less than a year after their marriage shows them seated under a pepper tree in Coronado, California—he, stunningly handsome in his Marine corporal's uniform, she, lovely and composed in a red and white checked cotton dress, a carnation corsage pinned to her shoulder.

Neither of my parents' families was pleased in the least by their decision to marry. Mother's parents thought she was marrying into a life for which she was completely unsuited, her college degree and artistic talent swept aside by the handsome, reckless farm boy she fell in love with. My father's parents were equally displeased. They couldn't imagine this pretty and refined city girl making any kind of farm wife. When my parents arrived in San Diego for my father's first assignment, they rented a room from another couple but soon got their own small apartment. Mother and the other wives met at the drugstore for coffee and wheeled their babies through the quiet neighborhoods, sharing their loneliness and their recipes. My father remembered his days in the Marine Corps as the happiest times of his life, but for mother they were slow, almost standstill days spent taking care of babies and marking time until my father was either sent to fight or to another base. My mother washed diapers out in the bathroom sink and hung them on a line slung between the kitchen and bathroom doors. For a few months they lived in an apartment up five flights of stairs, and later, hungering for company, she shared a small brick house with another soldier's wife. The woman's baby cried and banged his head on the crib for hours while the mother drank coffee and smoked on the back porch. When my father returned, they moved from that dark house, leaving the miserable mother and baby behind.

My mother's stories about these years tell me that from the time they were married my mother was present but not engaged, almost surprised by the life she was shaping for herself with each successive year and each new baby. As a child she could always be found at the neighbors or down the street, making up games or reading to other children, holding the babies while their mothers made lunch or did the laundry, and she was perfectly comfortable in our kitchen on the Tennessee poultry farm jostling a baby on her knee while she read the morning paper, or skimming the milk while we ate our oatmeal and toast. I saw her as completely competent and at the same time not really suited to the everyday demands that came from five children, a house, a garden, and two thousand laying hens. Maybe she was just exhausted. But it seemed then, as it did later, that she did those things she had to do with little investment, and even as a child I could feel her powerful focus, and full embrace of the moment when she was with a book or her paints. She painted all of her children, and the neighbors and their children, and the lush eggplants and ridged squash she planted and picked, and the hollyhocks and nasturtiums that grew easily by the back door. We took her work very seriously and walked quietly around her when she was painting. Walking in the door after school to the smell of linseed oil and paint told us that our mother, who worked with oils carrying names like cadmium red, ochre, cerulean blue and burnt sienna, oils reminiscent of Europe centuries ago, had another dimension than the cooking, cleaning, gardening mother we took for granted.

Like most girls of my generation, and that of my mother and grandmothers, dreams of marriage and babies had grown with me from childhood through high school and beyond. Our dreams of a future were precise and intricate, centered on falling in love with a man and getting married in a beautiful ceremony, having babies and a house. Our fantasies about the man we would marry filled our conversations during the sleepless slumber parties and the long afternoons spent lying in the sun slathered in baby oil and Mercurochrome. We imagined the color, texture, and cut of his hair, the possibility of him becoming bald never once occurring to us. His eyes were baby blue or coal black; his nose aquiline or noble; he was always tall and well built, not too skinny, never fat; he was going to be a doctor, a lawyer, work that would take him away from home every day while we stayed to bake and clean and iron, preparing for his return. He always carried a briefcase, wore a suit, coming from or going to his office. And we were the women in the magazines we read, wondering where we would meet this wonderful man who would provide us with a future, how to get him to notice us, how to make him fall in love with us instead of the conniving, manipulative and omnipresent "other woman" who lurked around the hors d'oeuvres at cocktail parties, or polished her nails at the receptionist's desk.

The men of my dreams, the men who had the starring roles in the movies and books my friends and I read, were professional, handsome, white, loving, rich, and far nicer, more successful, and more attractive than most of the men who actually came along. That was both good and bad. The dream image meant there was no need to settle too early or too easily and it propelled me out of Fernley, Nevada where the boys in high school were going to get jobs pumping gas or driving delivery trucks. This perfect man who shared my values would never think welfare mothers were a bigger problem than corporate bailouts or military buildup, and my plan to meet this man steered me away from the boys in my classes whose parents voted for Goldwater or who had patriotic bumper stickers plastered on their pickups. Of course, the men in my dreams did not have real opinions, certainly not any that would conflict with mine and actually, in this dream, I didn't have any strong opinions either. The perfect men who occupied the romance novels and movie magazines I read, however, also led to some problems in real relationships. They were so easy to be with, always loving, deeply devoted, as handsome as movie stars, romantic to a fault, never burdened by dull and dreary reality. Their energies were all spent on the romantic pursuit of me. There was no reason to ever give them up.

The Sears and J. C. Penney's catalogs offered a range of babies and toddlers, all white, from which to create our families, and my friends and I spent long afternoons designing our little paper moms and dads and children, always a baby too, selecting the clothes they would wear to bed and to school and to play from these pages. We decorated our shoe box kitchens with the refrigerators and stoves advertised in the catalog, and chose the dresses we would be wearing as we prepared the evening meal, waving to our husband through the kitchen window as he returned from work, whipping off our apron and readying the chilled glasses so he could make our martinis while the children played contentedly in the backyard sandbox.

In eighth grade in Wells, Nevada, I imagined myself to be Mrs. Brad Chamberlain as I rollerskated by his house, hoping to catch a glimpse of him. In high school, I tried on Mrs. Manuel Cordova, fantasizing marriage to a Paiute boy I longed for who lived on the reservation. I sat in classes in high school and college, trying out various married names for the boys or movie stars I fancied. Later in college, when it was clear that some boys were going to law school and some to medical school and some to the army, their futures were mine as I transformed myself from Mary White to Mrs. Somebody with each of them. Long before I married Kelsie, I had wrapped myself in Mrs. Kelsie Harder and found the fit a good one.

I was made whole by the identities of these boys and men, and in my images of the futures I tried on. I would be just who they wanted me to be, fitting myself into whatever life they built. I didn't only change my last name from White to

Whatever, I changed my entire identity. Losing my given name along the way was symbolic of becoming real, shedding the waiting and incomplete self for the self that belonged in the world. I would be subsumed, consumed, by a man who loved me. A man with prestige and power would seduce me; provide me with an identity that made me feel right, whole and real. I would find myself, my identity, my meaning (just as Eric Erikson the psychologist had said) when I knew who I would marry. Erikson didn't expect girls to have a strong identity. Theirs was to be relational rather than autonomous. I was going to be Mrs. Somebody Else and bear my husband's children and through these relationships I would *be*. Of course, growing up I had no real idea who I would marry, or how I would meet him or how I could prove he was the one. All of this was sweet mystery.

My grandmother Stewart knew that women of her class didn't have jobs, so there was no question that she would marry someone who could support her. At the same time, her relationship with my grandfather was built on romance and love rather than practical considerations. My grandmother White, who was orphaned as an infant, married because she wanted a place to call her own, a home and a family, knowing that she would never be "taken care of" but would live a life defined by hard work and struggle.

In the kitchen of our house in Wadsworth, doing dishes with my mother, I pleaded with her to tell me how I would know when I was in love, how I would know he was the right man, how I could be sure I wasn't making a mistake and there was some other man out there in the world somewhere who was really the man for whom I was destined. How could I avoid making the terrible, irrevocable mistake of falling in love with an ordinary boy from down the road when in fact God had destined me for a mysterious, urbane Frenchman whom I would meet on the streets of Paris, if only I could get there? "You will just know" she assured me, using the same words I used to reply to my daughters' entreaties years later. They were untrue when she spoke them, and by the time my daughters asked me I had been divorced three times, so I was pretty clearly not the best person to ask. When it came to knowing love, I was at as much of a loss as my mother and her mother had been.

I came to have love in my life only after three marriages and many years alone. It was a completely different experience from the cautious, self-protective, unre- vealing relationships I had with the men I married and with whom I was involved. I cherished his body, tall and strong, graceful and powerful, and loved his sweet smile and schoolboy haircut, his "scholarship shirts" with the frayed sleeves and collar. I adored his quirky ways—his pale pink plastic glasses which he had worn for twenty years, the sprinkling and streaking of gray in his charcoal hair, his perfect flat nails and strong calves—his little stories and jokes and his willingness to share with me his hurt and his losses. I was embraced and gladdened by his acceptance and appreciation, and my life was enormously enriched by his love. I took more risks, was warmer to others, less judgmental, more forgiving, more loving of my world, more open and confident. The transformative power of love, while diminished after we parted, was never obliterated.

My daughters, who grew up without their fathers in their daily lives, welcomed this man into ours. Knowing that I have loved someone fully has given my daughters the unquestioned knowledge that they can be loved and that they can accept the joy of being loved. I can bemoan the fact that I have known love only briefly, or I can celebrate the fact that I have known it at all.

I know many women, many of them married, who have never felt the deep, safe, warm connection, the trust and openness, the desire and embrace of love. My grandmother White never felt loved in her life. She and the other children in her family had been farmed out to relatives after their mother died and their father gave up trying to raise them on his own. She talked about watching her aunt kiss and hug her own children while my grandmother at age four and five stood by, longing for that embrace. "I always wanted somebody to show me love like that," she said. No one ever did.

I wanted Tyler's father when I first saw him. He was an artist, living in the tiny mountain town of Virginia City, in a roughly-constructed old house built into a hill overlooking a slag heap that strained toward distant blue mountains. He painted, he smoked, he drank and ranted, finding himself amusing and creative, knowing that others did too. He took himself seriously, he claimed the artist as an elevated status, demanding the right to be as wild and eccentric as needed to fuel his creativity. His confidence in himself and his art was captivating. We drank coffee and beer and listened to the Supremes coo "Baby Love" and I translated my fascination with his talent and his body into love. He had strong, square hands, blue eyes in a boyishly handsome face, a slow smile that escalated into a wild laugh or a raging growl. He was perceptive and smart, working endless hours drawing, painting, throwing pots, his energy electric. Only later did he become brittle, condemning and unforgiving, demanding that I join with him against the world he grew to despise.

The wedding was at our little brick house on Farm District Road, the house and fields coerced into beauty by the soft light of the late July afternoon. The lustrous field behind our yard served as backdrop for the wine and simple food displayed on fresh white tablecloths draped on temporary tables of plywood and sawhorses. My sister and I, along with my mother and her friends, had spent several afternoons making finger sandwiches and hors d'oeuvres, slicing crusts from bread, spreading them with pimento and cream cheese, sliced cucumbers and olives. Thirty years later, my mother, my daughter, my friends and I would perform this same ritual for Tyler's wedding. In the late afternoon light of our wedding day, the women wore pale yellows and soft blues and the men signaled the importance of the day by their serious white shirts and summer suits. In one of the photographs I have of myself on that day, I stand in front of an old fence, the startling green field behind me, hair swept up from smooth, almond eyes and heart shaped face, slim, elegant, young, and completely unaware of the meaning of that day for my life.

Kelsie had driven out to my house several months earlier, looking boyish and strong in boots, jeans and flannel shirt, and had given me a ring that his grand-mother had worn, warming me with the feeling that this thing we were doing made me complete and would usher me into the life I had been hoping for. I would soon have a husband and an identity. The pieces of my life were falling into place: I had been accepted into graduate school and was getting married, living at the edge of the new dream for women my age. I was not going to have to give up either of my dreams. I could have been a cover girl for the new feminist movement: You can have it all!

I pulled together all my hopes for love to walk down the aisle that day. I wanted to marry him and to have him love me. I wanted to complete the steps I knew would lead to happiness—husband, home, family. He was handsome and talented and intelligent and it was time to get married. I was afraid not to take this next most natural step in my life. I was also emotionally frozen, sexually inert, and terrified that I had spoken promises that now bound me for the rest of my life to a person I didn't even know very well. I was dismayed to realize one could be allowed to make such important decisions with so little preparation. Perhaps, I reasoned, my parents knew something I didn't about the process, or I was simply unaware of the way people were supposed to feel about marriage. The idea that adults, including my parents, whom I had always thought of as reasonable, sane people, concerned for my welfare, could encourage and participate in a life transforming event as if it were perfectly natural and normal, made the whole event seem unreal.

Kelsie and I remained strangers during the five years of our marriage even though we shared meals, decisions, holidays and, toward the end, a baby. We both came to the marriage without any idea of giving, of intimacy, and our inhibitions and fears were woven through our life together. The resentments he felt as I moved ahead with my graduate degree while he designed paper hats in a factory in Philadelphia, coupled with my guilt over his sacrifices, wedged us apart. We remained uncomfortable with one another, but constructed our obligation as a rela-tionship; he made my breakfast before I left for work or school in the morning, and I was happy to wash and iron his clothes. Despite the fact that our relationship was joyless, and that we both lived our lives internally rather than wrapped in one another's dreams, it seemed to us like an unremarkable, ordinary marriage. We were steeped in messages about marriage as sacrifice, discomfort and endurance; as long as these were present, the marriage seemed real, if not happy.

✶ ✶ ✶

Both of my grandmothers worked hard raising their children and making a home. Grandmother Stewart had the advantage of a well-appointed home and a graceful lifestyle, but she nevertheless did the washing and cooking and cleaning and all the other attendant chores for five children and her husband. She kept the house quiet so my grandfather could work on his sermons and she provided a comfortable place for him to visit with his colleagues and parishioners. My grandmother White never lived anywhere without a linoleum floor and hand-me-down furniture, and the meals she made for her seven children came from the garden she grew. Although their worlds were very different, the greatest difference between them was not that one was poor and one lived with more ease, one was rural and one urban, one had friends and music and conversations about books and ideas, and the other knew only family and church acquaintances. The difference was that even though they were both married for over fifty years, one knew love and one did not.

When my grandmother White (Mom) got married at twenty-six, at the turn of the twentieth century, romance was almost completely overwhelmed by necessity, a reflection of poverty so extreme that any dream was trampled by its leaden weight. Her hope for marriage was completely practical, built around escaping the dreary monotony of work in the fields, the kitchen, and caring for someone else's children. Her opportunity to marry came in a letter from my grandfather who lived with his uncle on a neighboring farm. He asked if, now that he had a little house and some acreage, she would marry him. A farmer needed a good wife and he knew my grandmother, Ada, and knew she would more than carry her weight. Her relief at being able to leave her aunt's house, especially her opportunity to escape her uncle, who forced her to wash his feet in a pan of water every evening and whipped her so often she ran away again and again, pushed her into a marriage that remained loveless and joyless for the next fifty years. She was afraid that she would never marry if she didn't marry Willis White. She was a rangy, raw-boned woman, with protruding teeth, awkward and unsure of herself. But she was strong and steady and she knew farming as well as my grandfather did. He, though dour and burdened by work and responsibility even as a young man, offered a life slightly less burdensome than the one she knew.

My Aunt Edna remembers that Mom's grandfather had promised to buy her material for a wedding dress if she ever got married, and when she received the letter proposing marriage, her grandfather took her into town to buy white poplin and ribbon from which she made her wedding dress. Married in February, they had the first of seven children by December, all of whom were to spend the first years of their lives in a sharecropper's shack. Their first child, Edna, who recently died at ninety-five, remembered the pain of having nothing and doing nothing but work. She illustrated her life by telling of one of the jobs she had when she was only four years old—to stand by the bed and push on the mattress to comfort my father who was a colicky and fussy infant. She stood, rocking the bed, until the pain in her legs and arms was so great that she dropped to the floor, crying along with my father. She never wanted children of her own and never had any.

Growing up, my grandmother was much more of a servant than a child, and she married my grandfather with the same matter of fact low expectations that she had learned to hold during all of her childhood. She and Pop married at a time when they were ready for the next step in life, and, in part, to get their own place to live and a piece of land to farm. Their courtship consisted of seeing one another on adjoining farms, playing together as kids, and eventually just walking together and going to church or square dances. My father's mother never spoke of feeling passion or longing or warmth for Pop, but she thought marriage would bring her happiness. If love includes passion, intimacy, and commitment, the only pieces of that puzzle she knew were tied to commitment. Marriage was, for her, simply what women did at a certain age, a continuation of work and caring for babies and making meals.

My father was the third child and the long awaited and much celebrated first son, born in 1916 on Island 35 in the mosquito infested Mississippi River. Unsurprisingly, my grandmother had jaundice throughout her pregnancy, but found no relief from the work in the fields, which she continued until the day my dad was born. A few months later, after finally saving enough money, my grandparents moved their growing family to a farm on dry land where they grew corn and cotton, and built their lives around work, family, church and community. They stayed on that farm for the next thirty years until Pop, ravaged by diabetes and the after effects of an accident that occurred when he tried to blow up a tree stump with dynamite, was physically unable to continue farming. Only then, after moving into a little tar-paper house on a dusty road in Advance, Missouri, did Mom begin to shape a life for herself. Mom seemed to decide that if she couldn't have happiness or love at least she would have some independence, and she finally decided: "I just kind of knew a little bit of what to do and what I wanted to do and I just kind of rebelled . . . I didn't feel like I was wrong."

Mom could have written all she had ever experienced about love in less than a paragraph. She had left behind drudgery and lovelessness for more of the same. From the beginning, my grandparents' marriage was built on hard work and obligation rather than warmth or intimacy, yet this was soon transformed for my grandmother into even greater emptiness and loss.

> *It got to where I didn't even like him, I guess that's the truth; it got to where I couldn't hardly stand him. He wanted me to leave and I just couldn't take it but I couldn't leave either. I had known him since I was a girl and I had Clyde (*her infant nephew*) to take care of and three other children by then. And where would I go?*

My grandparents were married for over half a century, and like many long marriages, theirs was difficult, distant and cold. One summer, Mom and I sat in her kitchen, my daughter playing with Mom's little scrap of a dog, and I finally asked this woman I loved so much and for whom I would have wanted the best, happiest, fullest life possible, if she thought Pop loved her. She told me about the night he died, after being in and out of the hospital several times during that last year. Before the ambulance came to take him to the hospital for the last time, he asked her, "If I don't come back what will you do?" After some hesitation and his insistence, she said, "I'll just stay here, Pop. It's home." He responded:

> *That's what I want you to do. I don't want you to let the kids get the upper hand to you, because if you don't, we got plenty that you won't want for anything, you know.*

"That," she said, "was the only time that I ever felt that he was interested in me."

Inez Tyler's brother, Will, introduced her to his friend, John Thomas Stewart, my grandfather, who had grown up within thirty miles of her home. He lived with his mother in the country, helping her take care of the old widower who owned the house and his animals in exchange for their room and board and speech lessons. My grandfather was a student at McKinley College, struggling financially, but determined to become a minister. Their courtship was slow paced and romantic, with long walks and talks and many hours spent alone or with friends. They were married when they were both only twenty after my grandfather promised my grandmother that she wouldn't have to give up her life of dancing, cards, and parties to marry a preacher. She insisted that she wasn't going to be a preacher's wife like other wives, and join the choir or go to the church circle. My grandfather agreed, asking only that she be a member of the congregation and go to church on Sundays. She expected love to lead to marriage and children and fulfillment, and that is what she experienced.

Inez loved my grandfather's mind and his gentleness, although he could be sarcastic and hurtful, shushing or criticizing her in front of friends or parishioners. Their relationship endured several of his rather public and humiliating affairs and some difficult economic times during the Depression, as well as the ordinary difficulties accompanying a big family, but my grandmother remembers their love and commitment, their happiest days coming after their children were grown and gone, when there "was nothing for us to fuss about." One of the darkest clouds hanging over my grandmother came when her mother moved in to live with them in their small house after her husband died. Her mother was only forty-nine, but, like so many widows, had "broken up housekeeping" after her husband's death, and spent the next twenty years with my mother's family, barely speaking to my grandfather, criticizing and carping at my grandmother, until she finally sank into a bedridden stupor, numbed by the laudanum readily available over the counter.

*She had been a beautiful woman, dancing, partying as a young girl, loving my
big, happy father. But by the time she died, she was a bitter old thing, demanding,
critical of how I raised the children, cooked, all of it. I know she must have been
in pain, and looking back, I know she was addicted to laudanum. Lots of people
were. The doctors just prescribed it for everything. She took to her bed about five
years after she moved in, and even though it was good to have her out of the
kitchen, her constant demands for attention, yelling from the bedroom, made me
feel like a slave. The kids had to go through her room to get to the sleeping porch,
and they used to wait until they thought she was asleep before they tiptoed across
the floor.*

Decades later my mother could still remember the smell of her grandmother's
room and the feel of her thin white hair in her hand when it was her turn to brush
it or pin it up for her. As my grandmother recounted this story, I thought of the
addictions that have ravaged my family, and wonder if my children have lived not
only the legacy of my father's alcoholism, but that of their great grandmother's
family as well.

My grandmother had refused to build her life around being a preacher's wife,
rejecting the restrictions and constraints, but she had nonetheless built it around
"daddy," and when he died she wanted to go with him in death, as she had followed
him in life. Friends and family could fill empty days, bring diversion, but the center
of her life was gone, and with it, her meaning.

*The children would encourage me to do things, and visit and call, and it was nice
to hear about them and the grandchildren, but it just didn't seem **important**. I
would just as soon not be around.*

And that is how she lived her next fifteen years after my grandfather died, dispirited
and dislocated.

While Inez found no reason for living after my grandfather died, my father's
mother, Ada, was finally freed by Pop's death, admitting with not a little guilt that
the best times of her life were the years she had after Pop died. She talked of the
simple freedom of time and the ability to make her own choices.

*Well, I've never had anything to upset or aggravate me and I do whatever I want
. . . so many times I couldn't do the things I wanted to do without I'd know that
we would have trouble. I didn't want to ever do anything bad. I always wanted to
do what was right. I don't know . . . I just kind of have been enjoying my children
more, and myself more. I have just liked it more since I've been on my own.*

Inez often entertained friends and visitors, serving coffee, pies and cakes she
had made, and cocktails in the evenings. She had the same highly polished and

carefully upholstered furniture all her life, and enjoyed sharing her comfortable home with friends, teachers and visitors. During any visit to my grandparents' house, we were constantly admonished to keep our feet off the furniture, our hands off the walls, our voices down, and our hands off the polished surfaces of the tables. I imagine now that part of her must have dreaded these five clumsy, ill-clothed children invading her tasteful rooms for the week or so we visited in the summers. We are now amused by mother's remembrance of her mother waving us goodbye after a visit, saying, "Helen honey, Daddy and I will really miss you and the kids, but it will be a good miss."

On the other hand, my father's mother never had a piece of furniture or dishes or linens that were anything other than purely functional. I don't believe she ever had a piece of silver or china, although she had beautiful quilts that she and the other women at her church pieced during evenings when all the other work was finished, or on church circle quilting days. The couch I remember was brown Naugahyde with a swirling, sweeping pattern squatting heavily on a linoleum floor, joined in the living room by a huge window air conditioner, a television and a plastic recliner reserved for Pop. His coffee can for spitting chew sat right by the arm. When I visited Mom a year before she died, we went to the general store in the little town where she shopped for groceries to buy a set of delicately flowered dishes she admired, probably one of the few things she ever let anyone know she wanted. Mom's pleasure came from her flower and vegetable gardens. The zinnias and marigolds I plant each spring hold her memory and I never pass a peony without thinking of our summer visits with her.

In the seventies I was teaching at the University of Missouri in Kansas City when one night I met Bob, Kate's father, who felt like my destiny. His outrageous wit and openness, coupled with an infectious childlikeness and vulnerability, over-whelmed me, blessed me, opened my world. Bob was tall, handsome, wealthy, funny, warm, and completely lovable. The fact that he had three children and I had one, that my job was terribly demanding while he was nearly retired, that he had a beautiful home and a housekeeper while I had a very modest apartment, that he had a Mercedes and I had a Toyota—none of this seemed to play any role in my assessment of our potential for a relationship. My theoretical clarity had no impact on my analysis of the misunderstandings we were headed for if we continued. I was thirty-one years old and eager for another child, and I wanted to love and be loved. This beautiful man came with all kinds of complications that I willingly ignored. I was living on two levels—on one, the mundane and weighty responsibility of teaching, research, and responsibility for Tyler, and on the other, escaping with him into late dinners at expensive restaurants, concerts, and parties.

I conceived Kate on a beautiful mid-summer night. When we made love that night, I felt a warmth, a fullness that thrilled me, convinced me I was pregnant. It is not just in the retelling or looking back; I knew it at that moment, the way women can know their bodies perfectly. Having longed to have another baby for several years, I think my body was poised for conception, eagerly waiting to warmly welcome the first hapless sperm that ventured its way. I reminded myself of Doris Lessing who writes in her autobiography that she had a tubal ligation because her drive to get pregnant was so overpowering she feared she would have spent the next ten years falling in love with men so she could have the experience of having a baby.

Being pregnant was thrilling, but the complication of having a real man in the picture was quite another thing. I had wanted a baby for so long, and had been willing to try almost anything to get one, from adoption to sperm donor, but the desire had been built around the baby, not the baby and the daddy. I thought Bob loved me, but I knew that he wanted someone to feel safe with, someone to take over his complicated and difficult life, someone to lean on and to partner with. I saw the fairytale life I had dreamed about as a girl in Fernley and Wadsworth and other backwater places come to life. I was a character in the story, a supporting cast member to his starring role. Despite all the struggles to get a Ph.D., the hard reality of a divorce, and supporting myself and Tyler, as soon as the right man came along, I fell comfortably into the role I had prepared for as a child. I was chosen, I was good, and I was worthy. I was woman. Thank you for making me whole.

The moment I was under the intoxicating spell of love, whose dangers I knew so well, the powerful messages of the 1950s, the comfortable images of femininity and masculinity that were so poorly suited for the life I was living, outmaneuvered my drive to accomplish and achieve for myself. I was completely overtaken by the desire to please, to be liked, to be viewed as nice and feminine, to be chosen and validated by a man. And he, of course, wanted a woman who was likable, compliant, warm and giving. I shared these conflicts with other women of my generation. New expectations and messages allowing us freedom and strength had been added to the formulas that were comfortable for us, resulting in both excitement and confusion. Our accomplishments were to be a "finish" for us; a veneer placed lightly over a core self that was deeply feminine, meaning nurturing, giving and essentially selfless in our commitment to being good wives. Men were, we had learned, strong, rational, unemotional and competitive, and they had learned that as well. So finding a man with these qualities, even in the extreme, was not difficult, and seemed for many of us to be the only kind of man there was. Men who were too nice, too gentle or too kind, as they themselves lamented, were not men we considered as potential partners. Women were trained to maintain the hierarchy we had grown up with, and to know that our place was below our partner, rather than above. We still expected him to make more money, to have a better job and to be decisive and rational, even as we were beginning to take on those expectations for ourselves, earning degrees and making our own money and decisions. There was bound to be confusion and conflict, not only between women and the men we were involved with but between the choices we now had and the powerful and comfortable constraints of traditional femininity.

On top of the powerful messages about purpose and meaning I had grown up with, coupled with the unremitting deep longing to have a baby, were the new expectations emerging within a different social and political context of the mid-to-late 1970s, messages about freedom and self-actualization and independence. The constraints and freedoms that informed the way we saw our choices were new to my generation. My mother would have had absolutely no choice had she become pregnant before she married, and would have joined the millions of brides who Betty Friedan wrote about going down the aisle pregnant. For my grandmothers, the condemnation would have been so great, and the choices so limited, that intercourse was virtually unthinkable before marriage. But the change in attitudes had been dramatic. I would not have been condemned by my colleagues if I had a baby without being married, and I certainly wouldn't have lost my job. Some of my friends would have applauded the refusal as a rejection of the "prostitution of marriage." My lesbian friends and friends who were very strong feminists would have seen single parenthood as the more honest, freer choice. Getting married was a bit retro, conformist. On the other hand, I was well aware of my grandmother White saying she could "just never accept a bastard child" no matter how much she loved me. And no matter what my politics were, how could I explain to my child four or five years later that she was not really "illegitimate" and that the word was simply a meaningless remnant of patriarchy?

Bob and I were married on a warm morning in early September, 1977, in a sedate ceremony on the dappled patio of a restaurant in Westport in Kansas City. Our guests were served crepes and champagne and both Bob and I looked far better than we felt. He was dressed in virginal white, while I, perhaps signaling my pregnancy, wore a soft beige dress that draped to my knees. His three sons and my daughter stood with us as we exchanged vows. Although we got married under less than perfect circumstances, the setting was beautiful, the food was perfect, and family and friends joined us to celebrate.

We signed our prenuptial agreement the day of the wedding, and the lack of trust in one another that implied simmered below our smiles. I took the ring he had bought at a little shop that sold ethnic bedspreads and incense burners as an accusation and a rejection even as I accepted it. Maybe I felt that was all I deserved since we both were entering the marriage with so many doubts and reservations that we had already spent time with attorneys and therapists, working through our expectations and trying to camouflage our fears. I entered the marriage knowing I was not going to meet his expectations; I was not going to give up my academic career and become the wife and mother for our four, soon-to-be five, children. He felt overwhelmed by the prospect of becoming a father again with his own three children being far from infancy and with a woman he knew slightly and trusted even less. I was thirty-two-years old, and while I reveled in the looks we got as a handsome couple with our stair-step children when we went out to dinner or to plays, I crumpled under the weight of the role. I felt like I was in the middle of a sieve, children, work, clothes, food, house, swirling around me as the part of me I thought of as *me* was swept down the drain.

I think we were both surprised by how quickly bitterness replaced the happiness and openness we had for such a short time but that had been so wonderful for us both. We were soon locked into rigid positions, becoming uncommunicative and distant, and we began to view one another as enemies—he seeing any softening toward me as a "win" for a woman who had trapped him by pregnancy, and me embracing every rejecting word and act as evidence of his privilege and assumption of superiority.

When my oldest daughter, Tyler, decided to get married the first time, neither of us had any idea that the decisions we made about her wedding, the idea of a wedding itself, could so powerfully pull us into morality debates, issues of values and class, illustrate expectations, and dredge up old hurts and disappointments the way it did. There seems to be nothing quite like a major milestone to bring up every piece of pain from the past, to interlace it with the hopes and happiness of today, so that every decision, every plan is heavy with history that threatens to overwhelm the moment. I was unprepared for the way this major transition in her life would reacquaint me with my past, reconnect me with my parents and grandparents. My sleep was interrupted with worries about caterers and invitations on one level, and with dreams about my former husbands, my childhood, and my daughter's future on another. My daughter's wedding returned me to my own wedding at twenty-one, taking the next and only reasonable step for a woman of my time. Walking down the aisle formed by the folding chairs in my parents' living room, I had been transported from that small brick house, that dirt yard bordered by wispy trees, suddenly submerged in the gentle rivers of time, joined not just to the man who would be my husband, but to millions of other women, to centuries of experience. Disappearing into the converging streams of countless marriages, I arrived at an identity that was normal and completely expected, and now it was Tyler's turn to travel that same path.

The wedding which introduced itself as an exciting event to be anticipated for months turned out to be, on further acquaintance, a disturbance of the past, a challenge to the peace my daughter and I had achieved through having tucked away difficult times. The wedding pointed out how fragile this deep mother-daughter bond could be. Yet, it finally brought us closer to one another as we recognized that the other choice was too wrenching—it was to let the past drive a wedge between us and trap us in isolation from one another at a time when our separation was inevitable. Our twenty-eight years together could be viewed with a mutual respect for what we had brought one another, or we could pick them apart finding every mistake, every wrong and every hurt we had caused one another. The hard work that we had to do required that we grow up—that I could hear what her life had been like without feeling accused and blamed and she could hear what mine had been without correcting me or resenting the choices I had made that shaped her world.

The deck would be the perfect place for the ceremony. It was oversized because I had it built to cover the swimming pool which provided more guilt than pleasure, winking its azure chastisement at us every day for its lack of use. Crowned with an arbor, the deck would accommodate the wedding party under a canopy of green provided by the lush trees, and allow seating for at least forty people, the rest would stand in the surrounding garden. Trees on the west and north would provide some shade, and we would keep the ceremony short to acknowledge the burning heat of a July morning. The yard would be beautiful, framed by fruit trees, ever-greens, flowering bushes, edged with roses and lilacs and flowering plum trees.

We turned our attention to the dress, or dresses. This was not as simple as it might sound, tied to questions about the number of bridesmaids, who they will be, who will be the maid of honor, will they "go well" together, what kind of dress will look good on different body shapes, and how much they should cost. This is of course just the bridesmaids. The cost of the dresses or food or music became mired, for my daughter, in her value as a person. I'm not the only parent that has felt that to hesitate when hit with the reality of the cost of the many unexpected expenses was like saying you don't value your daughter, you care more about saving a few bucks than about making this the proverbial happiest day of her life (the life that you have heretofore not done all that well with and this is your last chance for parental salvation). Not only do you need to weigh your daughter's value as a person and a loved child against the cost of the taffeta, lace and silk advertised in dozens of magazines for brides-to-be you now stumble over in her room, you have to buy the dress at the right store so that the entire experience is a confirmation of your love and her value. So, Macy's at the very least, but preferably a specialty shop, or maybe make a weekend of it and visit Nordstrom's in San Francisco.

The bridal gown was just one part of the picture, even though it was an important one. It would be the centerpiece of the experience, the fabric on which the entire event was built. My daughter dreamed of a wedding in which she wore a beautiful white gown, floated from the pages of a magazine onto a green sloping lawn, gothic towers in the background, crisply draped tables laden with succulent and exorbitant delicacies. Servants were to pass champagne on silver trays, every guest an elegant model draped in splendid finery. There would be gorgeous food that she would order but never touch, prepared and presented by the same caterers used by the people she knew who lived beautiful lives, fairytale lives, the only lives worth living.

I knew as she spoke about the dress, the day, the food, that there was no chance of matching the dream, and I remembered the many times I had tried to live the dream, always falling short, finally overwhelmed by anger at my failure or my daughter's refusal to complete the perfect picture I was making. For years I thought that if I just put all the right pieces together, I would have the feelings of safety and satisfaction that came from being in that picture. If the family was gathered around the dining room table on Sunday, we would all love one another, get good grades, have great friends, and walk in the grace of God. I was building the dream from the outside in, thinking if I just got all the parts right, the feelings that I knew those families in the Norman Rockwell paintings had would be mine.

I sometimes bristled at her wants even as I knew that this was a special day, supposedly the only time she would get married, a day unmatched by any other for her. I bridled not only at her unmatchable dreams and the realization that in the end, anything would fall short of perfection, but at all of the demands the day brought, how it glaringly revealed all of our imperfections, my flaws and failures. I was flooded by demands from every storybook I had grown up with and every romantic movie I had ever seen to sacrifice, to make this my daughter's most wonderful day, to give everything, to do everything right, to cut no corners in this display of love and acceptance. Even as I tried to swipe these images away, they gnawed at my consciousness and I felt both repelled by them and determined to fulfill them.

One big flaw in the fairytale picture I was trying to paint, of course, was that I was not married. Not only was I not married to her father, I was not married at all. Further, I had been divorced, not once, not twice, but three times. Despite the way that might sound, I had been single for over twenty years, since shortly after her sister's father, Bob, and I were divorced, when I rebounded into a three-month marriage with the principal of a Catholic high school who fairly quickly decided he was gay and moved to Las Vegas to work in the casino industry. The role of the mother of the bride is most comfortably tied to the father of the bride, hard to perform separately. It would have been so convenient and so commonplace only one generation earlier for the mother of the bride to effortlessly perform her minimal functions (she didn't even have to give the bride away). But in 1998, the mother of the bride was often an awkward thing, not completely sure of her role or function especially if her ex-husband was remarried. Not that it was so easy for the new wife, who didn't really have any role either, although she was vaguely tainted as the spoiler, trying to look legitimate, knowing all eyes were evaluating the father and the mother, hoping they would suck it up just for the day, maintain the pretense of the happy family for the bride and groom. Tyler's father was not even invited to the wedding. We hoped he didn't hear about the wedding, knowing that his presence would contort the day into a day with him, rather than her, at the center. Her sister Kate's father would come, and he came pretty close to filling the role, but he was Kate's dad, not hers.

Just as Tyler's dress symbolized perfection, the dress I was to wear became symbolic of everything I thought was wrong with weddings, marriage, and of course, myself. Mother-of-the-bride dresses relayed to me images of the faded sexuality of the mother, who was to wear a dusty rose color or pale beige, disappearing finally as a sexual and vibrant person, passing on any energy I had remaining to my daughter who was now to be given away to a young man with who she too would begin that journey toward eventual emptiness. I saw the dresses hanging limply in stores, waiting for a mother of the bride to settle on one as tolerable, not too sexy, not too matronly, not too flattering, sedate and solid, a dress in which she wouldn't completely disappear, but which, at the same time, would not draw attention to her. I saw myself wearing some brocade just-below-the-knee ashen-pink suit, topped with a hungry-looking corsage of carnations and lilies, heels sinking into the grass, perspiration spreading beneath my arms as I mingled with the guests, alone, probably drinking too much, smiling too stiffly. The image was intolerable and I insisted there would be no corsages for the mothers, and I would have a dress I could wear to other parties, casual parties, parties not so heavy with the weight of tradition.

Tyler's first wedding was fraught with the normal conflicts about issues such as seating arrangements, "giving away," bridesmaids' dresses, her wedding dress and the reception. The marriage itself lasted almost five years, and had some very sweet moments. It might have survived, even flourished, if not for a few insurmountable and completely predictable differences, exacerbated by youth and inexperience, as well as some pretty poor role models. Tyler, ethereal, dramatic, delicate, put aside her Bronte sisters and Virginia Wolfe to hike in the hills of eastern Nevada, hunting deer with her husband and his family. Rehearsals for a production in which she starred as George Sand were followed by a few beers and fries with Shawn and the guys from the construction crew at the bar near their house. He came home tired and a little tanked many nights and fell asleep on the couch watching television. She flirted with affairs—men who were older, completely unavailable or self-centered, romantic figures who were destructive and hurtful; men who were unsurprisingly like her father. She drove with her dog to a ranch in Wyoming, searching for a place to heal her soul, at the suggestion of a local humanities scholar who had gained as much notoriety as a ladies' man and an aspiring Native American as he had for his astute and intelligent performances of historical figures. These journeys took her farther and farther from her husband, her freedoms loosened her ties, unbound her and, in the end, undid her marriage.

Would her marriage have lasted had she lived with Shawn on a farm in Tennessee, bowed by work and the demands of children, or if she had had the support of a congregation, friends, and the constraints of a small southern town? I don't know. The parallels with my marriage to her father were sometimes startling. Shawn's mother, blond hair carefully brushed into a soft coif, little sequin-spattered jump suit, cinched at the waist with a beaded, silver, faux leather belt, was a slimmer version of Kelsie's mother, jaw set, eager to embrace any slight or wrong. She mentioned to several guests her dismay at our choice to have the wedding at home, in the garden, and to provide most of the food ourselves rather than having the wedding catered at a country club. What, with my income and everything. Shawn was strong, with soft blue eyes, and boyishly beautiful. The jeans and boots he favored could have been worn by Kelsie twenty-five years earlier.

After the wedding, Tyler, initially, was buoyant and open to all the changes in herself and others' responses to her, lightly creating beauty as she arranged their belongings, polished their silver wedding gifts, set the table with amusing arrangements and delightful food. The duplex where they lived, front door opening onto a concrete parking area, could, enhanced by flowers and fabric and books and candles, temporarily become the garret in Paris, the loft in SoHo she so badly wanted. But, in truth, even these, I believe, would have fallen short of her dreams. The delightful rooms she created were soon replaced by deep, hidden, emotional wounds, depressions that had plagued her since high school. Her depression led her to isolate herself in her darkened bedroom for days at a time, eating little, reading, sleeping and crying. Shawn was unprepared for the complexity of this young woman, her dreams of perfection unrealized. Tyler hovered between a convincing dance of competence and confidence, and a near-deadly misery, one melding with the other so seamlessly and with such rapidity that she seemed almost unreachable. Her exquisite beauty folded into a heavy pallor, deadening her features and slowing her movements. Her relationships were infused with the knowledge that she would transform from lithe spirit to sluggish corporeality with unpredictable regularity. The shadow of her pain darkened her relationships, making suspect, for her as well, the days and weeks she danced in the sun, imbuing her with fear of the happiness and the excitement, knowing it would crash into self-disgust and a deep need for isolation. Relationships built during the light could not be trusted to endure the long nights of despair, and she became reluctant to allow herself or another to hope she could keep the promise she exuded during the days and weeks of exuberance.

Several years later, Kate and I returned from Italy on a hot, windy evening, having spent the day in the airport in Turin, but enjoying, as a result, a full day in Amsterdam. Italy had been exhausting, both physically and emotionally. The splendid food and stunning beauty of the country was accompanied by unexpected difficulty traversing the language and coping with mundane demands of travel and lodging, and we had been overwhelmed by experiences we could never have anticipated. Kate was leveled by trauma and alcohol and fatigue, and I by my own exhaustion and vicarious suffering. Tyler and Josh met us at the airport with the car and the announcement that they were getting married on Sunday, only four days later. I heard their words, but was numbed by jet lag, lack of sleep, and the wrenching re-entry into the world so different from what I had just left. I had no avenue through which I could connect to this news on any level other than purely informational. The plans were already set in motion, and I was clearly going to be along for the ride, but not anywhere near the driver's seat.

The wedding would be at his parents' house; his father, a Lutheran minister, would officiate; they would decide on the flowers, the food, the guests, the wedding party and the clothes. Tyler was clearly struggling with what it meant to be getting married for the second time. She initially chose as her wedding attire a little beige, plaid suit that looked like it belonged in a Doris Day movie, tan shoes, the whole thing saying "I shouldn't be doing this but I am, so I will be as inconspicuous and appropriate as possible." No flair, no show, no "look at me, aren't I wonderful." Rather, "I am placid, I am stable, I am normal." "Sadie, Sadie, married lady, that's me."

I had, by almost universal agreement, a completely unreasonable investment in one thing: that Tyler keep her name, really *my* name. We had talked about it at length. I had peppered her since high school with the many wedding announcements in *The New York Times* in which the woman had kept her birth name. I rather shamelessly pushed her to see herself as one of those sophisticates, painting the women who didn't follow suit as backward and unfashionable. She had already changed her name once, to my great disappointment, and she knew that keeping her name meant to me that she was an independent person, had her own identity, and remained part of and connected to our family; that she did not subsume her identity in that of a man, merge with and become one with him. I had changed my name and Tyler's from Harder to Stewart, my mother's maiden name, a few years after my divorce from Kelsie, and I kept it through the next two marriages. My dad was hurt that I didn't take my maiden name, his name, back, but I didn't see myself as Mary Virginia White anymore—too pure, too virginal, too patriarchal. All of my twenty-five years of lecturing about women's studies came together in my desire for her to keep her name. It meant she was my daughter, that I mattered, that my values were central to her. I had kept my name when I married Kate's dad, convinced him to agree to hyphenate her last name to reveal her dual parentage, all of this a reflection of my deeply-held belief in the symbolic disappearance of women and the triumph of patriarchy in the practice of women changing their name to that of the man at marriage: coverture. I admittedly had a pretty big stake in this name thing.

As Tyler, the bridesmaids, the aunts, the groom's mother and I were crowded in the bedroom just before the ceremony, toasting the bride, she quietly and firmly told me that she was taking his name after all. I felt like I had been punched in the chest—a dull, physical pain. I was unremittingly unpleasant about it. I responded icily, claiming that she was abandoning herself, me, her dead grandfather, a century of feminist struggle, and her entire future. She ignored me completely just as she had a couple of days earlier when I told her I thought making six bridesmaids tramp through rocks and up the stairs onto a tiny deck and stand there in the hot sun in someone's backyard was ridiculous. I must acknowledge not being at my most gracious during this time.

The day didn't get any better after the ceremony itself, where I sat stiffly in the front row with Kate's dad, clenched teeth and disdainful eyes piercing my daughter's back. I found a good deal of solace in the white wine and was soon lumped against a wall in the kitchen, tears streaming down my face, claiming I had been abandoned by my daughter, that all of my sacrifices, all those years, the money on braces, on flute lessons, riding lessons, the private school, the seemingly endless hours at play and choir rehearsals, all were for naught, meaningless, lost in the embrace of a man she had known six months. And beyond that, he had the perfect family, not one sister, but three brothers and a sister, not a thrice divorced single mother but parents who were that very weekend celebrating their twenty-fifth wedding anniversary, not a disbeliever, someone confused about God and the ultimate meaning of life as a mother, but a father who was a Missouri Synod Lutheran minister, his wife a school teacher, their house in the suburbs. With unerring immaturity I took the entire wedding as a condemnation of my life, my identity, my being.

Neither Tyler nor Kate was in the least sympathetic with me. Kate kept casually sliding by me saying "**Mom,** this is not about you" or "**you** need to just get over it" and Tyler would periodically look up from some conversation or round of photos or the cake cutting, and give me a look of profound dismissal. At least I finally had enough sense to leave the wedding reception and go home. I spent the rest of the evening planning ways of ignoring Tyler for the rest of my life. In my mind, I took her out of my will, never spoke to her again and never saw the grandchildren she was bound to have. I built a life around retaliation for her rejection and then, I banished her from my deathbed. My resentments were only intermittently clouded by the knowledge that two days after the wedding she, my fragile, delicate, headstrong, hurt daughter and Josh would be leaving me, going to London where she would be teaching drama and English for a year. I knew I was being self-destructive and self-indulgent, putting distance between us at the very worst possible time for both of us, and I knew with certainty that I would miss her desperately, and worry about her, while at the same time I was being so venal I could barely tolerate myself.

The "good-byes" at the airport were a mixture of discomfort, sadness, and excitement. His family was cautiously polite to me, perhaps concerned that I would repeat some portion of my wedding performance. Tyler and Josh waved until we could no longer see them, Tyler jumping on a bench just before they rounded the last corner, and they were off.

I still think she should have kept her name.

I married three times, and each time I was driven by the idea that marriage would make me real. Bill, the man I married after my divorce from Kate's dad, had two daughters, a steady, unexciting career, and he offered predictability and a connection with familiar images of purpose and meaning to be gained through giving, serving, making the lives of others, him, his children, my children, perfect; taking them to dances, soccer, church, making them take their turn with chores, clean their rooms, do their homework. All of this felt like once more floating in that river of time with my mother and her mother and hers. I stood outside myself there in the living room that day, our wedding day, vowing to love and cherish the man I turned to after Bob made it clear that his commitment to our marriage was limited to "doing the gentlemanly thing." Our children and our guests gathered together, all of them more real to me than I was to myself. As I stood there holding my husband's hand, I knew absolutely that the emptiness gnawing at me would only grow, but the pull of solidity and a sense of finality carried me forward.

I was enamored of the idea of a complete family, his daughters and mine, merged into a family that would have Sunday dinners and vacations together, and I had hope that this would translate into love. Sometimes it felt like this was the way it was supposed to be, even though it didn't feel like love. It felt mature and valid. The package was right—the house, the daily round of activities, the cars in the garage, the children in school and me making breakfast, washing clothes, talking to teachers and neighbors. We went to dinner, to the theater, on trips. We shared friends. But he left after only a few months, moving out and leaving almost no trace of himself except that we were again alone. Tyler, only six, said the "sun shined through our windows again," and her words perfectly captured my feeling of freedom.

This same longing for normalcy has driven Tyler much of her life. Her marriage to Shawn was a deliberate step into a recognizable structure, but not so much as that to Josh. His minister father, homemaker mother, sprawling suburban house, brothers and sisters, spelled authentic, traditional and good for her. I think that same desire fueled her third marriage, as did her desire to have someone else make her whole. Her third husband, Terry, came with his own house, boat, other toys and four children, as well as a definite sense of masculine privilege and control. Here, finally, was a man who could tell her exactly who she was. I watched her being pulled toward his life, quickly abandoning her friends, her life, her possessions and her ideas. She forgave him his jealousy, his desire for ownership, control, anger and violence. She created a world in which she was mother and wife, which she translated as acceptable and legitimate, even as she married a man who beat her the week before she married him, and continued to beat her until terror and the certain knowledge that he would kill her if she stayed, drove her away.

It has to do with strength. I wasn't strong enough to be married and to also maintain an identity. I still might not be. The power and safety I feel alone unravels when my heart loops its ties around another. My youngest daughter, Kate, has a more grounded sense of herself and can, I believe, hold her own against the pressures to redefine herself in marriage. Perhaps this reflects her almost two decades of struggle with alcohol and drug addiction. Marriage won't undo her. Tyler, however, may be too fragile for marriage. She has struggled too often and too long with demons, mostly wretched products of her mind, and while she gains strength, she lives precariously near the brink of darkness. Tyler needed marriage too much. She needed it to shape who she was, to know herself, to feel value, to feel *there*. Perhaps she will have a good marriage someday, someday when she does not need it so much. Maybe I will too.

Inez's high school graduation photo, Du Quoin, Illinois, around 1911.

Inez with baby Frances, son Tyler, and her mother, Mattie, Du Quoin, Illinois, around 1919.

The Stewart children, Mary, Helen, Tyler, John Jr., and Frances, St. Louis, Missouri, around 1928.

Mom White with two of her daughters, Ila and Marie, Matthews, Missouri, around 1940.

Helen Stewart and John White, engagement photo, Coronado, California, 1942.

John T. and Inez Stewart, St. Louis, Missouri, around 1947. John was the religious news editor of the St. Louis Post Dispatch.

Helen at the breakfast table, Carroll Acres, Tennessee, 1950.

Family Portrait, Woodinville, Washington, 1953. John and Helen Stewart with all five children, Stewart, Johnny, Holly, Mary, and Geoff. Dad worked at the Irrigation Experiment Station in Prosser, Washington.

Holly, Mary, and Johnny on the "rock farm," Heck Road, Prosser, Washington, around 1955.

Mom and Pop White with their seven children on the farm near Matthews, Missouri, around 1958.

Helen with John at her graduation from the University of Nevada, Reno, 1965.

Mary and Kelsie on their wedding day, Fernley, Nevada, June, 1966.

Mary's research trip to southeast Missouri to interview her grandmothers, 1975.

Mary and Bob on their wedding day, Kansas City, Missouri, August, 1976.

Pat Gallagher feeding Katie, Kansas City, Missouri, 1977.

Tyler and Shawn on their wedding day, Reno, Nevada, June 1998.

Tyler, Kate, and Kate's son, Hudson, Reno, Nevada, 2011.

IV
Divorce and Disillusionment

My mother saw her mother's face blanch, saw her teeter and clench the back of the chair. She heard my grandfather tell her he wanted a divorce. And she couldn't believe he really meant he was in love with the high school art teacher, the woman who had just that evening come to supper. She wanted not to have heard what she heard. My mother remembers that my grandmother refused to entertain the idea, absolutely wouldn't consider it as a possibility, and fought both of them in every way she could. If she thought bribery would work, she would do that, if it took falling apart and spending a month in the hospital, she would do that, if it meant insisting she would saddle them with three of the children, she would do that. She simply would not be divorced. My mother's mother had five children, never worked outside the home and, as with all of her friends, had been groomed from childhood to be a wife and mother. She was simply unable to imagine a life without my grandfather as her husband and father to their children. Inez never revealed to me that my grandfather had asked her for a divorce, acknowledging only that their marriage was happier "after the children were grown." It would have spoiled the picture of the unwavering love she and my grandfather shared that she had recreated for herself as a widow.

My father's mother, who was miserable in her marriage to a man she had grown to dislike before her last child was born, never considered divorce either, but that was because she could not imagine survival on a farm with seven children without him. While my grandmother Stewart's identity was built around being the wife of a respected minister and mother of five healthy and successful children, she was also realistic enough to know she couldn't survive without his support. My grandmother White assessed her options entirely from a practical standpoint and saw no choice but to remain married. Later, she concluded that her life, despite this, had been better than that of most women she knew, in large part because of the joy she received from her children.

I believe my grandmothers, Ada and Inez, were willing to talk with me about intimate details of their lives, details they were often very uncomfortable sharing, simply because I so clearly and openly wanted to know. When I initially asked to interview them, they seemed surprised that anything in their lives could be interesting enough for me to travel to see them, notepad poised, tape recorder whirring, eagerly anticipating their stories about what they saw as mundane, prosaic experiences. My questions let them wander back through times they had not thought about for many years, pulling long dormant feelings into the present, filling the lives they now lived very much alone with the voices of their children and husbands. The past became present for them during those days we sat in their living room or kitchen and talked. Inez was once again making meals for "daddy" while he worked on his sermons in his upstairs office, hidden beneath a dark cloud of cigar smoke. She took her laundry to be washed and ironed by the woman down the block, and raised her children in a small mining town, then in a crowded city apartment. Ada was again standing on a kitchen chair to wash the dishes, learning to quilt and can, making meals for the field hands, learning to give her children the love she had never known.

Mom was a big boned, lanky, warm woman and people were easily drawn to her. If she was shucking corn or shelling peas, the grandkids wanted to be doing it with her. If she was going to the field to pick corn or was out working in the garden, whatever she was doing, the kids wanted to be right beside her. Pop was jealous of her and the attention people gave her, even when they were old and the risk of her leaving was long over. He didn't mind her learning to drive the tractor but he didn't want her learning to drive the car and he was sullen and angry if the guy at the gas station was nice to her, or the man next door waved hello, or if she went anywhere by herself. She accepted the constraints of her marriage as inevitable and built her life around her children, grandchildren, and her church, providing the services my grandfather expected as an obligation, but without feeling.

Mom's relationship with her children was strong and intimate and her disappointment with her marriage was something she simply put up with. She talked to me about her long relationship with my grandfather, with little display of emotion.

I would try to keep the quarrels down but he just loved to be in little spats all the time. I think he would just like to criticize what you done. Then I would get mad and say things I shouldn't. He wasn't all to blame, but he just didn't have any respect for me.

Her voice flattens as she remembers her unhappiness:

He was just bossy and he'd curse me in front of the children if something happened. He treated me like I wasn't worth much and he told me what I had to do and I had to do it.

Mom didn't ever love Pop the way she thought she should, and over time, she grew to not even like him. Maybe, she suggests:

because he had to work so hard all the time to make a living, we was never close to one another and we never had fun. I respected him because he was my husband, but I didn't really love him like I should. I never did.

Yet, she never seriously considered leaving him. Her life had been so constricted since childhood that she had no sense of a different life for herself. Even when she thought of leaving, she was limited to going to family, and there being none who could take her, she felt trapped where she was. The idea that she could have gone off on her own, even before she had all seven children, leaving her aunts and uncles and the familiar hardships to risk a new life was unfathomable to her. Her life was constricted by place, lack of education, culture and gender, and by circumstances she saw as immutable.

When my grandfather died, my grandmother was freed and she spent the next fifteen years happier than she had ever been in her life. She answered to no one, read her Bible, watched television, went to church, enjoyed quilting with her friends and did exactly as she pleased.

I hate to tell you this, Mary, and maybe I'm wrong, but the last fifteen years since Pop died have been my happiest. I just never have anything to upset me or aggravate me and I do the things I wanted to do. Before, I knew we'd have trouble. And I didn't want to ever do anything bad.

My own mother was completely unprepared for the life my father offered. She approached it like she was walking into a cold wind, steeling herself against the relentless farm work and isolation that was so foreign to her. Just after they were married, my parents moved to the farm my father's parents had near Matthews, Missouri. For the first few months they lived in the house with Mom and Pop and their two youngest sons, who were still in school. One evening at supper, a conversation quickly became a heated argument about race—my grandparents were both as racist as were most poor southern whites, and the language they used offended my mother deeply. My father stood by my mother and that night they moved out with my brother, who was less than two, and me, under six months. An old shed that had been a sharecropper's shack stood at the back of the garden, and they were able to fix it up enough to make it livable. They got along better with the rest of the family with a little distance between them. Mother still had to go up to the house to pump water and to use the ice-box, but she was happier there in her own place. I think about this reality, bringing people from such different backgrounds together under one roof, as it contrasts with our romanticized, inaccurate images of the extended family.

Pop assumed that anything that happened to his boys or on his place was his business. One day, when I was about two, Mother bought me a little maroon coat with a matching fur-trimmed hat and muff. Seeing this new outfit, Pop intoned, "Well, well, Helen, you and John sure must be making a lot of money." My mother resented his intrusion, but on the farm, as long as Pop was alive, John was his boy, and Pop called all the shots. If mother and dad had plans to go into town on Saturday morning and Pop heard about an auction he wanted my dad to "carry him to," going to town with Mother would just have to wait until the next week. It was not long before the clash between my mother and my grandfather encouraged my father to look for a job that would put even more distance between them, and soon they moved to Carroll Acres.

My father's father, sour and bitter, demanded respect rather than affection from his children. My father's mother, on the other hand, offered unqualified love and warmth, particularly to my father and his brothers. Because my dad loved his mother so openly, so generously and unabashedly, so much that he would do anything she asked, including building an indoor bathroom when Pop insisted the outhouse was good enough for anyone who wasn't uppity, my mother thought he would be as loving and warm with her. But, like many men, his love for his mother was a thing apart, and my mother was the "wife," expected to take care of the kids and kitchen while he drove the tractor and milked the cows. Making sure no one had any reason to look down on his family meant a lot of hours in the field for him and a pretty firm commitment to my mother "knowing her place," even though he really didn't know quite what to do about it if she got out of line other than complain and cajole. Dad got over that view as he got older, and encouraged my mother's painting and political work, helping her hang her work in shows, showing off her prizes at the county fairs in Tennessee and later, in Reno, collecting signatures on petitions with her in support of Cesar Chavez and demonstrating against segregation in front of Woolworth's.

By the time my parents finally divorced, I was twenty-five, married with a baby and on the brink of divorce myself. My sister was also married and living in New York, my older brother had married, finished law school and was practicing in Reno. My parents talked more and more often of divorce, especially during times when my father was drinking and my mother was angry or simply fed up with the marriage, the debts, the worry, the life. In the towns where we had lived the only jobs available for women her age were "postmistress," waitress or prostitute. When we moved to Reno and she returned to college to get her teaching certificate after Johnny, Holly and I were on our own, she was clear with my father that she would divorce him as soon as she could support herself. In a few decades, the options for women had changed dramatically—whereas my grandmothers wouldn't, and really couldn't, consider divorce, and my mother was middle aged before it was an option for her, by 1970 the generations were converging, with my mother and I, twenty-five years apart, divorcing at the same time.

We children felt like the adults during my parents' divorce, believing them to be mistakenly rushing into decisions for which they were utterly unprepared. My mother spent weeks sitting in front of the television drinking vodka tonics after work. My father moved into a tiny, dark room in a hotel near skid row as if his surroundings had to match his mood. My brother, Stewart, pulled himself into an emotionally self-sufficient and affable young man, determined to mold a smooth and successful exterior life, banishing even the possibility of divorce from his future. Geoffrey, the youngest, was angry, bereft, incredulous, scared. His misery lasted through his final year of high school. He was furious with my father, was impatient and irritated with my mother, and accused my father's new wife of being a home-wrecker. Years softened his feelings and today his relationship with my dad's widow is strong and supportive.

The divorce was much harder than my mother had expected. For almost a year, she seemed in turn aimless, angry and depressed. At the end of that year, she decided to move to San Francisco. I don't believe she ever imagined that so much time would pass before she became the person she had prepared to be, that twenty-five years would come and go before she was no longer poor, living on a farm or in some drab, small town, going through all the motions of raising a family and being a wife, separated from her feelings. Her identity had for many years been completely entwined with her children and my father. She was, as she said, our mother and John's wife, but had no sense of who she was on her own. San Francisco was a theater piece, a play in which she had long yearned to perform. She was completely free of her children, beginning to move again in her world as a woman, as sexual, smart and attractive. She used the lump sum alimony payment from my dad to buy a house in a marginal, moving-up neighborhood and taught in a community school where the teachers pretty much ran the school, left alone by the principal and the school board. However, after ten years of teaching second graders to read, she left teaching, sold her house and used the proceeds to transform a five-bedroom single family home into a bed and breakfast inn. She was creating a showpiece, gutting and renovating the house, choosing the fabrics and paint, carefully selecting furniture for each room, and planning and planting the English garden. Designing the inn was as creative as painting had been when she was younger and the realization that she could put together an acceptable business plan that a bank would back was revitalizing and self-affirming.

I don't believe I have ever known my mother to be happier, or to be more self-involved, than she was then. Her children were both proud of her and angry with her for having something more important than they. I resented terribly her attentions to men she fell for when I wanted her to nurture and pet me when I visited, pregnant with Kate, divorced, and caring for Tyler, who was only five. She would rush out of the house at night to meet Tony or another man, leaving me there, wanting her to be the grandma I imagined her to be, knowing now that I will not completely fulfill my daughters' expectations of "Grandma" either. She was living her life without consideration for her children or their needs or judgments, and she loved it. We visited her world, admired her, and tried to reconcile this mother who had many friends, stayed out late, had affairs, and plowed through all sorts of financial problems and bureaucratic hurdles to build what she wanted to build for herself, with the mother we had known baking bread, working in the garden and being there for us. She didn't ask for our advice or approval, and in fact acted as if we were too backward to really participate in the sophisticated world she now inhabited.

Twenty years later, when she sold the inn she had babied and nurtured and moved back to Reno, reconciling the woman she was in San Francisco, the competent urban sophisticate, with the grandmother and mother we anticipated her to be, was no easy task. We moved right back into expecting her to be our mom, and she struggled with her love for us and her grandchildren and the feeling of being discounted by these children, all busy professionals who seemed to place their lives and their needs above hers. From successful businesswoman, respected political activist, and charming, sexy woman, she now was considered "mother," not just by her children, but by people she met with her children. She had left Reno so that she would be Helen, not Mary's, or Holly's, or Johnny's, or Geoffrey's mother, and now at dinners, or political or social events, she was often just that again, and while she took pride in our accomplishments and appreciated being identified with us, she once more felt dismissed as a person in her own right. My mother is one of the most accomplished people I have known, but despite all of her successes and all the ways she expanded her life and became so much more than just our mother, she does not cherish memories of, or long for, that time in her life. When I visit her today in the Alzheimer's care center where she lives, what remains at the core of her being, what sticks with her as other details blur and disappear, is her deep, solid love for her children. As I put my hand on her arm to gently wake her from a nap several days ago, she woke, surprised to see me, and began touching my face, petting me actually, and saying, "Mary, I love you *so much.* You are so beautiful, I *love* you." It has been a gift, though a terribly sad one, for me to watch my mother as she is changed by her disease, and to see that her love and tenderness for us are steadfast and unwavering.

My mother didn't remarry after her divorce, and never regretted it, foreseeing herself wiping the chin of some old man and helping him with his pajamas and heart medicine. My father, on the other hand, remarried immediately after the divorce, proposing to Barbara, a woman he met at an AA meeting. All of us children were not so much rejecting as unbelieving. His marriage to another person besides our mother seemed like a careless game he was playing, one that would end when he and my mother realized the significance and consequences of ending their marriage.

Years ago, my former husband wrote to me that he would marry the woman he lived with when "things settled down around here." I am fully aware that we never make the big decisions in our lives when things are right, when all our ducks are in a row, when all our plans are laid. Some people, like my sister, and me in different ways, rush headlong into marriage or move from one continent to another with no more than a glance into the future. How else would I have three such short and unsuccessful marriages behind me by the time I was thirty-three? Others are so cautious, so burdened by doing the right thing from the perspective of all the people who are affected, that they are paralyzed. There is never a good time, a perfect time, even an acceptable time for major change. It is always going to be a bad time, a hard time, a difficult time, a lonely time, a painful time . . . these are the right words, the only conceivable words, for any time tied to such upheavals in life.

Decisions that change your life, especially when they require so much undoing and disentangling, cannot be done smoothly, with no ripple. You cannot decide to dissolve a marriage and think you can meet the morning as if you had not just violated promises you had always meant to keep, caused pain for people you would never want to hurt, as if you hadn't pulled apart, torn apart, the world you had all agreed to keep together. When you decide or know that you will move the walls of your life, undo the latches, open some doors and close some, this cannot be done without wailing and blaming and wanting it to not be true, hoping it is a nightmare erased by the morning. This cannot be done quietly, with calm dignity and mutual appreciation, at least for me. Someone is violated, someone is left, everyone is hurt in different ways. The storm cannot be avoided, the destructiveness, the power of such a blow, cannot be denied. And maybe as we get older, we fear this pain more, we have so many more layers to peel. We may also fear the unknown and unpredictable; we cannot imagine waking to unfamiliar sounds and sights, getting the paper from a different porch, putting our key in another lock. We bring to any loss a storehouse of losses which have gone before. Knowing how much we can hurt, and for how long, we may be desperate to avoid it, while at the same time, our knowledge that we lived through what we thought was unendurable pain, even thrived, gives strength, and for some of us, even a glimmer of excitement as we face the unknown. We know that loss is not only loss but that it also holds seeds of promise and hope, often deeply hidden.

Until we know we must change, we are pulled by such contradictory forces that we are left immobile. When everything is possible, when everything carries joy and hurt in equal measure or at least in balanced measure, we remain where we are. There is no movement until there is imbalance. Sometimes this imbalance, this unsettling tilt in our lives, comes from small tears and bruises that begin to loosen us from our moorings. These imperceptible changes, each alone lacking in depth or bulk, slowly erode who we were and reflect to us someone with whom we are not altogether familiar. Sometimes, we suffer strong and damaging collisions that we could not have anticipated, from which we fear we will never recover, but which are slowly absorbed, becoming part of us in a powerful, invisible way. But whether we are marred by small and repetitive lacerations, punctured by deep gashes, or are ignored and unattended, our bodies and our souls begin to change—they are pummeled into a new form, shrivel and turn in on themselves, or laboriously drag themselves into a new shape.

Sometimes these changes sweep across us like grit in a sandstorm, roll over us like killing waves, accompanied by noise and blindness and fear which overwhelm us. They tear and shred and pull and batter us. We can try to avoid the maelstrom or we can steer straight into the gale, not skirting it, because that is the only way to get through it. You can turn your back on the rage of rain, but the wind shifts and catches you unaware. You can wait it out, and it will pass, but as long as you are walking across the same desert, or navigating the same ocean, it will find you again.

There was no way I was going to have a twenty-five year miserable marriage, or even a mediocre one. And I knew I had moved beyond the constraints my mother experienced; supporting myself was no problem, and being a single mother was not nearly as stigmatized as it had been when my mother was young. Not to say that my timing was all that great. I divorced each time when my babies were infants or newborns, placing me in the unlikely position of having been married three times but having always been a single parent. This brief history of marriage makes me cautious in the assessment of my daughters' marriages or plans for marriage. In only four generations, the pattern of divorce for women in my family has changed dramatically, from virtually no serious consideration of divorce for my grand-mothers, to a wrenching divorce for my mother after a long marriage, and shorter marriages, three divorces, and long periods of being single for me. I would not wish the constraints of my grandmothers' marriages on my daughters, yet neither do I encourage them to model their decisions on my own.

One semester, a lively young woman who was a student in one of my Women's Studies classes told me she was going to drop the class. She explained that she had recently married and she couldn't both remain married and remain in the class. She saw the analysis of marriage as accurate, she felt constrained, her identity submerged, but she also loved her new husband and planned a life with him. The conflict was too extreme for her to handle. Even though I could not articulate it at the time, I believe that the choice I made was the opposite; my analysis of marriage didn't allow me to comfortably fit within it, yet I had never imagined myself alone. At the same time, I had worked so hard to get where I was that I couldn't see giving it all up for marriage. There was no real possibility of sustaining both a marriage and the work which involved such a critical view of it. It was almost impossible to critically analyze the power structure of traditional marriage, to see the restrictions on women's lives, and to feel comfortable within those constraints at the same time. It was impossible to hold the beliefs I did about the oppressiveness of not only marriage, but of all institutions in the patriarchal system, and to comfortably remain in an inferior position within them. The fact that conflicts between two worlds were so clearly drawn, the gap so wide, made the decision to divorce both simple and wrenching.

My determination not to give up the deep feeling of authenticity and satisfaction I felt with my work, and my completely unanalyzed, seemingly "natural" desire to be married and to have a family were far more incompatible than I could have imagined. I thought I could live my life on two levels, achieve the dreams of marriage, babies, love and happiness that accompanied me from childhood and still succeed in this new world of work and obligation. It was absolutely absurd, shot through with unavoidable contradictions. When Bob and I married, he thought he was marrying a woman who would be the wife he wanted, who would care for his children, his home, *his* needs. He assumed that I would become the perfect housewife, effortlessly grocery shopping, washing and folding endless loads of laundry, cleaning our house, *his* house, cooking meals that were largely unappreciated, and being a sweet and loving stepmother to his boys, none of whom were thrilled with me being thrust into their lives. He let his full-time housekeeper go, and we agreed to take turns with the morning routine of getting the kids up, fed and ready for school on time. Of course, Bob's schedule was much more flexible than mine; he would go to meetings over lunch and stop by the office for a while to take care of some business, while I was teaching full-time, grading papers, writing articles and doing required research and scholarship. I felt myself bristle each time he would sleep in on mornings it was not "his turn." It was not only his assumption that I would do all these things, *be* all these things, that infuriated me, it was my unquestioned and automatic compliance with these expectations that left me seething with resentment and confusion.

My desire to be a good mother, to have the children like me, ran head on into my frustration at having to ask them repeatedly to set the table, or to help bring the groceries out of the car. Every morning that I scraped ice off my windshield, I blew frosty, vile accusations at Bob, asleep upstairs, his car warmly tucked in the garage. I put my clothes away in the one drawer and about a foot of closet space Bob had cleared for my things and eyed his closet full of cashmere and wool and freshly pressed pants with a withering rage. I hated him for calling from work, then from a grocery store, then from a friend's, having me wait dinner, then getting home and asking the kids if they wanted to go out. I listened to him praise the "warm, loving, giving" waitresses and clerks, watched him carry other women's bags and open their doors and pulled farther away from him and more into myself. Any woman who didn't have a job, or a good job, any woman who was a nurse, or a waitress or a full-time mother assumed the status of near-saint, depicting me, I thought, as self-absorbed, hard, cold, ungiving, and unloving. To be woman was to sacrifice. There was no way I could live dual, contradictory lives; minor adjustments would have no impact on the deep fissures that divided me and separated me from my husband.

I felt that peace and comfort, even if not accompanied by happiness, could only be achieved by giving up one enormous and demanding part of my life, and I chose to give up marriage. I had anguished much more over the decision to marry than over my decision to divorce. I knew a decision to stay in the marriage was a decision to abandon myself and at least half of my dreams, even as these con-tradicted the hopes and expectations that had coiled themselves around my heart from childhood. Later, when the children were grown and I had the tenure and the status that I had worked for, I wondered if I would have been happier, felt more whole and real had I remained in my marriages. I could leave my marriages because I knew I could support myself and my children. I also knew that I wouldn't be ostracized or condemned by most people, and I knew that I could handle the work on my own. I left all three of my marriages knowing that a large part of my identity came from my work and my relationship with my daughters, rather than from my relationship with my husbands.

The only way the divorce rate wouldn't have increased after the women's movement is if it had been legally prohibited or if the consequences of divorce would have been intolerable, as they were a century earlier when women lost their children and all of their support when they left their husband, no matter how good the reason. The critics of the women's movement couldn't have been more right—it ruined marriages, split up families, destroyed dependence, encouraged women to take their children and start their own lives. And at the time, all of that seemed good. Most of it still does.

The women's movement of the 1970s had uncovered the inherent problems built into marriage—its legal and social inequality. Divorce and single parenthood were identified by many women as superior to the oppressiveness of the traditional marriage. The rhetoric merged with and shaped my analysis of my own marriages, making the prospect of being alone with my children seem brighter and happier than remaining in an unfulfilling marriage. In contrast to my grandmother Stewart who gained her value through making my grandfather's life better and easier, I wanted that easier life for myself; I wanted someone to see my needs and desires as important. The obvious problems with marriage reflected the juxtaposition of the child's heart, molded by the songs and stories of romance, which promised safety and a known and predictable future, with that of a woman who had grown to want the openness of the unknown and the possible.

I shaped a life for my daughters that was far different from the one I had known growing up, and I did so at some expense, not only to myself, but unknowingly, to my daughters. Although I was immersed in messages that justified and validated divorce in my academic world, I knew almost no one in my "real life" who was divorced, certainly none of my parents' friends had divorced. I was unprepared for the unease I felt about being divorced, which held heavier and different implications than just being "single." I had expected to feel liberated and satisfied, proud of the example I was setting as avant-garde and enlightened, but all of the images I held of myself as an adult and as a mother included two people, a couple or pair, and I struggled to reconcile the image of who I thought I was going to be, with the reality of who I was now.

While divorce marred the picture I had of myself as an adult woman and happy mother and wife, it also offered a cool and open emptiness that was a welcome replacement for marriages which felt tight and airless. During this time of separation and reconstruction, I had what passed for emotions; deep demanding wants and a great reservoir of determination and strength. These were all above the shoulders, cognitive and powerful. Expectations and goals, hard work, doing the right thing and avoiding failure replaced feelings. Whether it was school or love or work, I seemed to *accompany* me rather than to *be* me. I existed on two planes, the "me" who was resolute and tenacious, and the "me" who was really experiencing the loneliness, the doubts, the confusion and worry. Only with my babies, my girls, did I exist completely. Leaving work in the afternoons to take the girls to the park or for ice cream provided me with a feeling of wholeness, of being right in the world. There was no contradiction between being a completely engaged mother, buying the best Buster Brown shoes, the sweetest Winnie the Pooh dresses, and being the woman writing articles about sexism and misogyny. The conflict was completely between marriage and the work I did, marriage and who I was.

Kelsie and I lovingly put together our baby's room during the months before she was born, picking out colorful fabrics, and sanding and painting furniture that friends no longer needed. I made yellow dotted-Swiss curtains to match the bright quilts and blankets we had received as gifts. The living room, the kitchen and our baby's room form a clear memory for me; our bedroom is in shadows. Neither of us was miserable, but we were too young and inexperienced, we didn't know how to be the husband and wife we were supposed to be. Kelsie would stop home for coffee and a visit mid-mornings while delivering the signs he was painting for grocery stores and other businesses. We cooked rice and chicken back casseroles or baked vegetable and cheese casseroles from the surplus food we got with our neighbors, either at our house or theirs. We spent many evenings with our friends Kathy and Griff Durham on their back porch, barbecuing, drinking and smoking, caught up in the moment while still keeping one eye on the responsibilities of tomorrow. We became like family, sharing not only porches and backyards with one another, but also ourselves—our humor and silliness. Our evenings of laughter and conversation buoyed me and kept me above water in those months.

But, most evenings I worked at our kitchen table, the air heavy with cigarette smoke, drinking countless cups of coffee and giving all of my energy, my focus, to completing my Ph.D. I read endless books and papers and worked on my dissertation, constantly researching, revising, restructuring. My body and my mind were strained with fatigue, yet I was relentless, dogged in my efforts to achieve my goal, to actually have something tangible that would establish me in the world as successful, smart—*somebody*.

When Tyler was born, I was still fully immersed in my work, determined not to let motherhood prohibit me from becoming Dr. Mary Harder. Yet, when our delicate and fragile daughter arrived, I was transformed into a mother. I remember vividly my astonishment at the nurses' cavalier attitudes as they handed me my baby and ushered us out the hospital doors. Were they crazy? What kind of people would let me just take her away without any experience safeguarding and caring for this tiny person? I thought surely I was missing some kind of information that was handed out to other mothers, and that my ignorance would result in sure disaster.

Kelsie and I learned what to do, how to sing and cradle and comfort. I learned that Tyler wasn't as fragile as I had imagined, and I became a bit more confident in my ability to be her mom. I was becoming familiar with my daughter's sounds and gestures, I was falling in love with her, and yet the tie between Kelsie and me kept loosening. We were still drifting near one another, inhabiting one another's space but not connecting. It wasn't that I was not loved, or that I was not loving. It was my inability to find a way to navigate through the messy turmoil of our complicated love. Kelsie was also unable to mend our frayed bond, unequipped to allow feelings for me or Tyler to intrude on the deep isolation he needed in order to create his art.

I had already been accepted into a graduate program when Kelsie and I married, so the fact that I was going to get a Ph.D. should not have come as such a surprise. If school had been something I did that didn't impinge on his life at all, we wouldn't have had the problems we did. And if school and a new baby had been happenstances, events occurring on the outside edges of his life, we wouldn't have had the problems. But, mixing all of the expectations of school, Tyler, and the house, while still stumbling around what it meant to be a wife, created a blur of demands and fatigue. When I tried to sort the jumble of books and diapers and meals and being married, marriage fell out.

I left him one morning, taking with me only a few belongings. I remember taking only my baby, who was six months old, and the coffee pot. The precipitating event didn't initially seem that determining. A few days earlier, during a very cold early spring week, against Kelsie's wishes I had gone to visit my mother in San Francisco, taking Tyler. He was angry at being disobeyed, which is the right word even though it seems unreal to say it, but promised to meet me at the bus station on our return. The bus ride home was especially long because of heavy snowfall and Tyler was wakeful and fussy. When we finally arrived around midnight he wasn't there to meet us and my phone calls to him went unanswered. The station was by now almost deserted, and I kept a watchful eye on the suitcase and diaper bag and blankets as I went back and forth from the phone booth to our pile of belongings. Still, no answer. Finally I took a cab home, lumbered up the stairs, dragging all our luggage, and found him sleeping soundly, peacefully. That finally closed the door for me. I was wretched with anger at his insensitivity, and in the heat of rejection and fury, feelings of hopelessness cascaded around me. The trap of struggling to be acceptable, adding one responsibility on top of the next to make things work, to be loved, to be good enough, was pried open, and I walked out. The sudden knowledge that I was basically on my own, even with a husband, torpedoed whatever remnants of allegiance I felt to the marriage.

The low-lying fog that hung heavily over our marriage lifted when I left, but hovered above us rather than clearing. I was surprised at the ease with which I could leave the man I had married, our house, our life. At the same time, I was filled with guilt for hurting Kelsie, for taking his daughter, for not being there for him. Nevada and most states still relied on the "tender years doctrine" assuring women that they would keep their babies and young children after a divorce. Kelsie had been there through the pregnancy, he had walked the halls of the maternity ward, miserably powerless, hurting for me during a very hard labor. He thought our baby was the most wonderful baby the world had ever seen. And I was willing to take her from him, not because I wanted to hurt him, but because I was leaving him and it never occurred to me that I would not take her with me. She was *my* baby.

Knowing that a marriage was unworkable and knowing that a relationship was unhealthy didn't translate into being free from it. I remained linked to Kelsie for at least the next decade, through two more marriages and several jobs. In part I was trapped by the loss of the image of protection, warmth and realness that accompanied my picture of marriage. The images that replaced this picture were sketchy, only dimly lit. And the reality of living in a tiny, one-bedroom, furnished apartment was less than I had hoped for. The brown plastic furniture, dark green carpet and table pushed against the wall would depress me if I woke to them today. Yet, they were enough for me then, all I needed—bare, spare, and plenty. Tyler was with a sitter while I was in class, and after a few hours together in the evenings I coaxed her to sleep in her crib and worked at my desk until early morning. Being there felt wrong and empty and thoughts of the warmth and familiarity of his body, his hands, ate away at my resolve, challenging the reason for my leaving. What selfishness was this, what purpose did this serve? The powerful condemnations of women who were selfish, who put their own needs ahead of those of their husband and children, were deeply embedded in my brain. The power I had to leave, to take my baby, to start on my own, seemed like a lie, like something I shouldn't be allowed to have. Where was the order? Why was I able to unravel our relationship with my will, my decisions? Why hadn't someone who knew better stepped in and told us what to do, how to make it right again?

Before I had completed my dissertation I was offered a position at the University of Northern Colorado and I took it without a moment of thought. I had gone to school to get a Ph.D. A person with a Ph.D. taught at a University. There was no question. In August, 1971, Tyler in arms and a few belongings shipped ahead in boxes, we flew from Reno to Greeley, Colorado. The fact that this flight was my first, at twenty-five and her first, at almost one year of age, foretold the enormous contrasts between her generation and mine. We moved into a furnished house and I began a year of teaching and more long hours finishing my dissertation. I taught more courses in one quarter than I teach today in a semester; I labored over my dissertation, prepared my classes, wrote papers and squeezed in some time for new friends and romance. I walked Tyler in her stroller; we went to the park, stopped for ice cream, visited friends along the way. The University had a child care center and I was finally able to get her enrolled. I spent the first day she went uneasily, knowing she would be scared or unhappy with all those new faces in a new place. When I arrived to pick her up in the late afternoon, I was both excited to see her and fearful that she would be miserable. She was sitting at a table outside with several other children laughing and eating Jell-O. A huge burden of guilt and worry was lifted.

While the separation and divorce from Kelsie had been emotionally wrenching for both of us, and while we were ugly and jealous with one another, accusing and hostile and hurtful to one another, in Greeley, our relationship began to be the long-term destructive force that it would remain for over a decade. I think that his anger was the most solid and reliable thing in my life and his burning rages grounded me in the familiar past. I could pick up the phone, imagine him there at his drawing table, ink pen in hand, or in his studio, painting, having a few beers. I was trans-ported from a lonely, plastic mannequin to a despised, dangerous, powerful and sexual woman through his toxic raging and tormented attacks. My sense of myself was ensnared in his distorted perceptions of me, but at the same time, I knew that he couldn't possibly think the picture he drew of me was accurate. I discounted the words and went for the meaning, one I constructed out of my own needs rather than one he presented. The words that bruised my ears somehow soothed my heart. I longed to hear them. The vituperative attacks could only mean he cared about me, that I was the star of his show. I went to bed at night strangely warmed by the knowledge that a tangle of hurt bound him inextricably to me.

Though he was hundreds of miles from me he was ever-present, filling my days and nights, blocking any possibility of someone else becoming real to me. Marina Tsvetaeva, the exuberant, brilliant, passionate Russian poet who wrote during the Revolution, concluded that absence and longing were superior to happiness. To Boris Pasternak, the pivotal figure in her emotional and intellectual life, she wrote, "My favorite kind of relationship is otherworldly; to see someone in a dream. And the second is correspondence." As her biographer Claudia Pierpont says, "She had finally learned to beware the flesh, the loss inherent in consummation." The predictable, maybe formulaic emotional upheavals of the letters and calls from Kelsie were sustaining. I could suck from him powerful feelings that I internalized as connection and closeness and never have to face the mundane or practical realities of having a relationship in everyday life.

I suspect I have always known that the destructive relationship I maintained with Kelsie, even after our divorce, was also destructive to my daughter, even as I justified it in terms of her need for a father. He punished Tyler and all three of his daughters, each time they gathered enough strength to ask for his love, refusing to forgive them for being their mothers' daughters. His rejection of his daughters left wounds so deep, so untouchable, that these daughters never fully recovered. All three of these young women have suffered enormously, and in different ways with the passing of time, wrapped in a longing that dims their spirit, eats away at their core of self-acceptance, making them vulnerable to the waves of inadequacy and worthlessness that sweep away accomplishments and successes, requiring them to begin the hard process of rebuilding over and over again.

I think Kelsie could simply not believe that I would leave him and take our baby out of his life. Because I had left him and taken his child, Kelsie felt no responsibility to help support his daughter. This wasn't so unusual and it didn't occur to me that I could force him to. In fact, since we didn't live in the same state, I probably couldn't have, and only much later, when an attorney presented me with the absurdity that if I didn't try to collect child support I could be seen as a "neglectful mother" giving my former husband grounds for a custody battle, did I resort to legal means to get support. This was largely unsuccessful, again because of jurisdictional issues, but for a while Kelsie paid support to the state ($50.00 a month which even in 1973 was laughable) and they sent me quarterly payments. Most men didn't pay child support mandated by the court and the mandated amount was usually inadequate to begin with. Almost all of the single fathers had a similar justification; it was her choice to leave and he had no obligation to support her, or his job was not good enough to allow him to help out, or he had more pressing concerns, or was between jobs, sometimes, of course, staying unemployed, or underemployed simply to avoid paying. So women got custody, but our income levels dropped substantially. Then, like now, the hardest part of divorce for most women was the economic and emotional hardship they faced as single parents.

I came to my second marriage with the same drives and needs that had laced my unhappiness with Kelsie, needs that were bound to be unmet. I felt transformed by the knowledge that someone loved me, wanted me, especially someone as handsome, as articulate, and as witty as Bob. He was a perfect fit with the romance magazines that had occupied so many warm summer afternoons in Wadsworth. He was drawn to my self-assurance, my competence and what looked to him like strength. These were the very qualities that began to erode as I became enamored of him. The more I cared for him, the weaker I became, the more connected to him, the less I knew who I was.

Bob probably had every reason to believe I would continue to be the accepting, nurturing and patient woman he saw during the early days of our courtship. Instead, even before we got married, I began to resent not being cared for, being the mother, the nurturer, instead of the loved one. I was solid, dependable and responsible, to the exclusion of qualities of lightness and openness which had also been a part of my character. I was back to being the Mary of my childhood, watching out for Holly, taking care of the other children, making sure everyone was happy, being background. But now it didn't feel comfortable. Just as I had realized with Kelsie that it wasn't enough to applaud his talent, I realized that the road I was on with Bob wouldn't accommodate any plans I had for myself. I began to feel the same slippage I had felt with Kelsie; the marriage would work if I could fit comfortably within the rhythms of his life, caring for him, his children and mine, the house. But that meant walking away from teaching, writing, and tenure. I couldn't easily give up plans for a career when "the perfect man" came along, so the romance was tarnished, the dream broken into too many incompatible pieces to survive.

I'm not sure either of us thought about what the outcome might be in the long run, whether the distance we put between ourselves so early could ever lessen, or what our current misery meant for the future. We had pledged "till death do us part" standing there on that lovely patio with friends and family, and two weeks into the marriage we were barely speaking to one another, maintaining a charade of marriage in front of the children, sleeping with our backs to one another on our new firm mattress, driving our separate cars to the marriage counselor, leaving alone. The oldest boy, convinced that I had trapped his dad into marriage, dragged himself through the house sullenly, came to the table with uncombed hair, unbrushed teeth, a sheet wrapped around his body, both he and his father watching to see if I would comment. The other boys, ten and fourteen, approached me cautiously. I was a virtual stranger, inserted into the middle of their lives, making them dinners they didn't want, awkwardly talking about their homework or bedtimes, trying to impose images of wife and mother that came directly from some 1950s television program I didn't believe in and they hadn't ever seen. Tyler was completely lost, overwhelmed by the unspoken misery in the house, knowing she had no way out on her own, deciding to shelter herself from our anger and disappointment by disappearing into herself.

I refused to even consider giving up my profession, not only because that would signal capitulation to the traditional demands of motherhood, but in part because I was a mother, and was going to have another baby. I was overwhelmed by my work but at the same time wrapped in the safety it promised, the identity it provided. The fear I felt at losing what I had was palpable. To give up my work meant I had made a mistake leaving Kelsie. To give it up meant I would have to trust Bob, trust marriage, trust a man. Being alone for me was far less frightening than knowing I depended on someone else, someone who could leave, leave me.

If I had been willing to loosen my tight hold on what was mine, my work, my safety, he may have been willing to trust me enough to begin to love me. If he had been willing to love me, promise to care for me, I may have been willing to let go. We were unmovable, and increasingly distrusting, uncommunicative and hostile to one another. All the issues with Kelsie were there again; if there was no guarantee of being loved completely and compellingly for the rest of my life I would risk nothing. Bob and I agonized and avoided and hurt one another for months. We made love. We had long talks in which we revealed little. But, without absolute assurance that he loved me, wanted me, and was committed to me, I could not stay with him. There is something weak about demanding so much—all or nothing at all. Love me completely or I will be alone. A stronger person would be able to build more out of less, to need less from another and rely more on herself.

This struggle reminded me so much of my desire before Kelsie and I were married for him to tell me he loved me and that he wanted me to stay with him. Since he wouldn't, I decided to leave, to go to Temple University to graduate school. I have yet to find a person who thinks the bargain I wanted to strike was fair to him. Yet, I was simply unable to give up the opportunity to take care of myself, which I assumed I could do well, without a guarantee that someone else would be always solidly in my life. I would be lonely and afraid and angry, but I would not feel resentful and abandoned.

And I didn't *just* want marriage. My parents were married and unhappy, as were my father's parents, either for long periods of time or for the duration of their marriage. I wanted love and commitment and romance, and absent that I wanted to be on my own. Always the pull between work and love, always one part of me longing to simply be cared for, to fall into that place of peace where I thought so many generations of women had lived, with another part of me just beginning to feel myself, to feel freedom and competence and fearing to abandon it. Yet, if a man that I loved promised he could somehow guarantee me that he would always love me and I would always love him and we would never leave one another, I would have given up everything else for him. But who could make such a guarantee? What looked like headstrong independence on my part was only partly the knowledge that I was competent and able to take care of myself and my children. At least an equal part was fear of trusting anyone else with my life and fear of being trapped in a situation in which I would be miserable and would have no choices. I had watched my mother, like many women of her generation, wait until the children were grown and then divorce my father. But the quarter century they were married seemed to me like a lifetime, and I found even a year of misery to be intolerable.

Perhaps it was something else altogether, a reflection of the changes brought by the previous twenty years. For the first time middle class women like me, women who were not among the elite, could live well on our own, have children, friends, a home and a life that mattered. To relinquish that possibility, that promise, called for another promise, one that was completely unrealistic within the context of that time; the promise of complete and endless commitment. Rather than having only one approved, promising path to follow, now there were two, one more familiar than the other, but both with real possibilities for fulfillment. Maybe our devotion to the notion that we could do it all, have it all, came from the fear of having to choose. Better to try to mesh these, actually blend the new with the old and established, than to risk the unknown. But such a merger could not be made, in fact, and one had to face the choice. This necessarily brought torment just as it offered joy. This personal misery was, I believe, a manifestation of the collision of too many conflicting expectations, histories and needs that so many of us brought into relationships, these being fueled by the swift fire of cultural change erupting in blazes beyond our control.

Despite the fact that by the late 1970s everyone was well aware of the dangers smoking and drinking posed to a fetus, as Bob and I spiraled into miserable mutual resentment, I embraced bourbon and cigarettes like long-lost friends. I loved smoking, and the drinking seemed like a justifiable punishment, a symbol of misery and loss. My associations with alcohol were almost all negative. That is what drew me. I recognized the damage I was potentially doing to myself, and to my baby, the self-destruction, even though no one had yet talked about fetal alcohol syndrome. I sat for hours in a spare bedroom and smoked and drank and thought. I taught during the day, and prepared my lectures and even worked on articles; I got up with the children and got breakfast when it was "my turn," and I was a civilized and involved parent. But, when Tyler was finally in bed and Bob was out, as he was almost every night, I sat alone and hurt myself and my baby. After only a few weeks of this, I pulled myself out of that misery, knowing I could not continue the destructive behavior, that I would be better on my own. I think Bob was more humiliated by the fact that the neighbors could see the moving van in the driveway and guess what was happening than he was upset that I was moving out. He was probably as lonely as I was and felt as unappreciated and unloved as I did.

By Thanksgiving I was gone from his grand, well-appointed house, pregnant with our baby, and comfortable in a tidy white frame house, windows shuttered in red. Kansas City was gray and cold in early November, and it was raining when I met the rental agent at the house. I wore a loose, heavy jacket, thinking she might have reservations about renting to a single woman with one child and now six months pregnant. All the stereotypes about single pregnant women gathered around me as I waited for her, and I silently beat them back. The house was perfect; gold carpet, white walls, a sun porch off the living room, and a tiny, tiled kitchen with a back door leading to a small yard where Tyler's swing set and toys could be placed. Upstairs there were three small bedrooms and a bath, exactly right for us. The house was small, cozy, on a quiet street and the neighbors were either retired couples or young families. The trees played games with the sun on the walls, and the feeling of comfort, closeness and warmth convinced me to rent it. I waited anxiously for a few days while my references were checked, carefully avoiding mentioning that I was married, hoping one of Bob's children wouldn't give me away if the agent called. When I was approved, I eagerly paid the first and last months' rent and then tried to figure out how I would tell Bob that I was leaving him.

Although there were many similarities between my first two marriages, the second one looked very different from the first—we were older, I was pregnant, we both had children, we were already involved in our careers and we were each financially stable. Despite these obvious differences, the problems that arose for us were actually the full-fledged displays of the incipient problems Kelsie and I had faced a decade or so earlier, and they emerged in a culture that was the culmination of the sexual revolution, the anti-war movement, and the women's movement which were just beginning to twirl around us when Kelsie and I got married. The feminist movement, which was fledgling in the mid-1960s, had become a powerful force politically and in academia. Feminists challenged marriage as an institution that was oppressive to women, a form of prostitution in which women sold their bodies for economic support from their husbands. Betty Friedan was encouraging women to get out of the home, to get jobs, for their own sake, but, more importantly, for the sake of their children who they were smothering, feminizing their sons with their overbearing attentions and manipulations. Gloria Steinem, who later married for the first time at sixty, happily concluded that "a woman without a man is like a fish without a bicycle" and she was beautiful enough and accomplished enough to be believable. Our identities were not to be dependent on our husbands or our children. In fact, having a husband made one's feminist credentials somewhat suspect. For that matter, being heterosexual raised the suspicion of being "male identified" and made one questionable as a legitimate feminist. My friends and I found Phyllis Schlafly, Lionel Tiger and George Gilder not dangerous, but laughable. Tiger justified male privilege on the basis of primitive male bonding, Schlafly intoned that women gained more power from dependence than independence, and Gilder warned that society was being driven to "sexual suicide" by the feminist movement.

This was the era of the "no-fault divorce" system that allowed either member of the couple to "dissolve" the marriage, no questions asked, buttressed by the assumption that they would both start out again even. The assumptions were laughable because, of course, women leaving a marriage, especially after being home, let's say for twenty years raising the family, were in no position to compete in the marketplace and to support themselves as well as their husbands, who had been moving up the ladder during that same time. Yet, if women were awarded any settlement, it was often "rehabilitative," a term that, oddly enough, seems to reflect an assumption that marriage was inherently damaging or crippling for women. Even though the judges and pundits insisted that men and women were equal and that neither should be "punished" by their "irreconcilable differences," women were very likely to lose a great deal financially. If women wanted equality they would "get what they asked for" with the no-fault formula. In addition, no fault divorce often assumed equal sharing of custody and parenting, when, in fact, most of the time women still had the care and custody of the children (unless the man wanted custody, and then he was very likely to prevail) and supported them on far less money than their ex-husbands made. He wasn't any more likely to pay child support than he was under the old "fault" system, and if he did, he often didn't pay it for long, or pay enough to support the children.

I tried to put my grandmothers in my place. They had never considered a career. They had not had the option of leaving, being alone with their children without suffering poverty or ostracism. While they couldn't divorce easily, neither were they likely to be left. My mother? Realistically she couldn't leave with five children. She didn't have a career. While my grandmothers either accepted their marriages with their imperfections, or didn't have any other choice, they didn't seem to be resentful like my mother was. And I, refusing to be resentful, refusing to give up what I had worked for, unbending and unyielding, could be alone with my children. For better or for worse.

I settled into the little white house with Tyler while Bob and I tried to pull our relationship together long enough to get through the birth of our baby. We weren't divorced yet, and made cautious stabs at working things out, making little progress given my insecurities and lack of trust, and his anger at me for first trapping him into marriage and disrupting his life, then not being a warm and loving wife, and ultimately, embarrassing him, after he had done the "gentlemanly thing." We took childbirth classes together, an almost laughable failure. He didn't want to touch my body, which I felt was pretty untouchable and unlovable in the first place, so he went through the breathing exercises himself, along with all the pregnant women. The other men were doing the fingertip massage on their wives' ballooned bellies and gently adjusting pillows and blankets for their wives while Bob was attentively following instructions, counting and doing "pant-blows" of his own. After our weekly class, we walked to our separate cars and went to our separate houses. At the end of the pregnancy, my sister came to be with me, and when serious labor began, she called Bob, who came for me and bundled my little suitcase and me into his car for our trip to the hospital. He stayed during the entire labor and delivery, adjusting the music, changing the stations, chatting with the nurses, entertaining whoever might be up for it, and finally cheering me on through the delivery. I have never seen a happier man. Labor was relatively easy, and short and we were both thrilled with a perfect baby girl. The fact that we couldn't agree on a name for her for weeks, and that we even changed her name on her birth certificate, from Margaret Holly to Kate (finding an agreeable middle name would have been unthinkable) about six weeks after she was born illustrated the amount of conflict we still had in our relationship and the misery we were willing to endure to not give in to one another.

Having a baby brought us closer together only slightly and only temporarily. I had gone home from the hospital to my house. Bob visited frequently at first, then decided to wander off to Mexico in search of himself. My closest friend, Pat Gallagher, who had been with me since Tyler was a baby, took Tyler to school, helped with the housework and took on much of the mothering, while my sister spent long hours in the kitchen, pampering me with recipes she'd gathered on her trips around the world. Meanwhile, with Pat's and Holly's help, I ate wonderful meals, rested, nursed my baby, loved my little Tyler, and was as content as I had ever been. My colleagues covered my classes for a few weeks and I returned only for a month or so before I was able to take the entire summer off. Bob and I continued to make stabs at reestablishing a relationship, me wanting him to love me, him asserting his continuing doubts, until finally it became clear to me that I had to stop waiting to see if he would ever want me, and to decide for myself that it was over. We were both relieved.

My relief was short-lived. Bob began to suggest in subtle ways that he wanted custody of our baby. His reasoning was perfect, and perfectly consistent with the new "no-fault" system that assumed that the custody should go to the parent "most able to provide." Of course, in most situations, if "provide" was defined financially, the man, if he so chose, would be at an enormous advantage because he was, in part due to the wife's economic sacrifices, in a much better financial position. I had more money than most women, but not nearly as much as Bob. His argument was that I had to work and he didn't, and I would have to hire a babysitter to come in whereas he could just have his housekeeper watch over the baby the few times he had to be away from her, and he could give her benefits I would find difficult given my economically disadvantaged position. I argued that were he willing to provide more child support any financial advantage he had would be erased, but I couldn't deny that I would have to have a babysitter. All of my arguments were really beside the point. I simply knew that I would not give up custody of my baby. I had longed for her; week after week I had followed her while she developed toes and fingers and ears and eyes and I was never going to give her up. I think Bob knew that the fight would simply not be worth it, and he agreed to a modest child support and we finally were divorced before Kate was a year old. Kate has never lived with her father, and to do so would seem strange for her. When she was about eleven or twelve, Bob and I traveled a little together with her, and got along so well that Kate was alarmed, worried that we might "get together," an idea she found astonishingly unacceptable. How could you be in love, she wondered, you're my parents?

I met my third husband through our children and their romantic dreams were folded into our decisions about the future. The problems were obvious; he moved into my house, he had two daughters and I had two daughters. We were both very accustomed to living on our own. Much as I had been when I married Bob, I was overcome by the heavy weight of marriage. One Sunday, sitting in the Lutheran Church with Bill and our children, tears would not stop. The image of myself, mother, wife, churchgoer, good American, was so oppressive that I almost could not breathe.

The only difficulty I had removing myself from this third marriage was the embarrassment I felt, for example when the Lutheran minister would visit to talk with Bill and me about our religious beliefs and our marriage. My beliefs were rather tangled and difficult to articulate and our marriage was a sham that I maintained for many weekly visits, until I finally simply admitted Bill was gone, never to return, at which point so was the minister.

I disappeared under the heavy hand of marriage. With my children I didn't lose myself, either in them or in motherhood. The role of *mother* wasn't developed broadly enough to include single parenthood, and the many of us who were divorced and single with children were free to find our own way, to be mothers to our children without assuming an identity that demanded the abandonment of self. But the wife role wasn't so forgiving. Wives were to be good and loyal and giving and warm and self-sacrificing and responsible. Sex was an obligation, not an offering. Mothering within marriage came with rules, and the highly embellished vision of family imposed itself on the unwary in a way that often crushed the spirit.

For better or for worse, divorce from one's husband, of course, doesn't neces-sarily end the relationship with him. For me, these ongoing relationships have been, in one case, devastating and destructive to my daughter, Tyler, and to me, and in the other, supportive and positive for all of us, at least after a time. However, that isn't to say that remaining in any of those marriages would have been a better choice. Tyler's father's almost macabre ugliness to her is a reflection not of the divorce, but of his character, and illustrates the reasons a divorce was for me, and I believe for her, a far better choice than remaining married. Kate's father, Bob, while no better a husband than I was a wife, shares with me a love and caring consideration for our daughter that has helped us remain close. The first couple of years were hard. The fact that the marriage didn't work didn't erase our complicated feelings for one another. He remarried just months after our divorce. At first, I was angry and jealous, but with time, we both began to see the other as allies rather than enemies. The woman he so quickly married had a lot to do with that, and, despite my tangled feelings, I was able to acknowledge her wisdom and appreciate her presence. She made it clear to me and to Kate, who was just a baby, that she wasn't Kate's mommy but that she was a reliable, trustworthy friend married to her father. She was the most mature and level-headed of all of us. I never really thanked her for that, probably because I didn't know at the time the importance of what she had done.

Many years later, when I had been single for fourteen years and my daughters were nearly grown, I met a man whose caring for me was deep, whole, unreserved, uncritical and completely giving. Geoff was the first man in my life to completely embrace me emotionally, to know my doubts and inadequacies and to see these as simply being a part of a person he loved. We cooked together, taught together—he helping me more than I helped him with articles and projects. He took Kate to her horseback riding lessons and picked her up at school when I couldn't. He was a solid, good, intelligent person. He was a completely dependable friend, a gentle and thoughtful lover, an intellectual companion, and a deeply caring, spiritual man. I didn't love him.

I bridled under his caring. I wanted out of the relationship that was too close, too wrapped up, too final feeling, and I was unappreciative and often burdened by guilt. During those brief moments I was married to Kate's dad I had similar feelings. On our wedding day, we were actually taking a nap, both of us having been up almost all night hammering out the prenuptial agreement, creating lasting resentment in the process. He gently turned to me and said, lovingly, "It is so good to have a wife." Instead of sinking into the blissful security of couple-hood, I immediately envisioned a large corrugated aluminum sewer pipe into the side of which were cut covered, locked windows about every twenty feet. At the end of the tunnel was a locked set of double doors. That was how I felt on my wedding day. Small wonder I was living on my own again within three months.

By March of my second year with Geoff, waiting until after his birthday, I finally left the relationship, knowing it wasn't what I wanted and wishing it was. I felt free, relieved and satisfied. I didn't miss him for one moment. I didn't long for him one time. I was happy to have closed the door, to once more be clearly on my own and to look for someone to build something with. I was again ready for the struggle that made me feel alive, grounded, real. In late summer, we unexpectedly met on the library stairs and my heart began pounding heavily. I lost my balance, my skin was clammy, my tongue thick. Looking at him, I was overcome with loss and grief. For the next few weeks I slept only fitfully; I longed for him. I wanted to call him. I felt shredded inside, raw.

While before, with him, I had yearned for my own time, had sought solace in long, hot baths, the closed door a silent rejection of him, now I wanted to touch his arms, stroke his chest, have him desire me. While I had talked lightly, carelessly about the importance of separate bedrooms if we were to live together, now I wanted him to spend every night in my bed. I felt I could only be whole if he would have me, love me. I was desperately afraid, and I wasn't sure why.

One summer night, he finally agreed to come to my house for a glass of wine and to talk. I had called him earlier in the day, feigning a casualness I could only sustain for the few minutes I was on the phone. Fear edged with dread prowled heavily through my day. That evening, we found seats facing one another on my new redwood deck, the wood still soft and golden. Pulling myself close to him, I found myself stroking his arms, caressing his fingers, remembering the pleasure I took in them during lovemaking. I fought my desire to demand that he love me, come back, be who he had been to me. Achieving a calm I didn't feel, I asked him to come back to me, revealing my love, my desire for him in a way I had never done, being completely vulnerable to a man who had been so willing to care for me. He refused. He was resolute. It was too late. He cared about me but was no longer in love with me. It was over. None of this seemed real. He had been there for me through so much, never wavering, always willing. There must be something I needed to say or do, some particular thing that would reach him so he would soften and come back to me. I couldn't accept the possibility that he would not. He would not.

For the next two years, I seemed able only to move through the day to get to the night to get to the day again. It was baffling. I could communicate with other people, go to dinner or a movie with my friends, be productive at work. But all of this took place on the smooth, flat surface of my mind, while inside I was knotted and snarled. I was so accustomed to being split, to looking fine and happy and feeling empty and dead, or seeming present and feeling like I had vacated myself, or looking competent and feeling self-loathing, that I could move in my world as if I were there. But my hold on myself was very unsteady. Today, the feelings of loss and longing have let go of me. I still don't understand exactly why I sank so low at that time, why I was thrown into such loss and worthlessness so suddenly and so deeply and why I finally emerged from it, after so many dreadful months. Pieces of it are clear. Both of my children were gone; one in Europe and one away at boarding school. The silence was profound. Here suddenly in my late forties, I was stripped of the immediacy of the relationships that had held me together. Our work and families and homes had merged; we knew every conversation the other had, every deadline the other met, what foods and fabrics the other liked, and every plan. We talked several times a day, had lunch together, drinks after work, dinner. He was always there. We gardened together; the lilacs I see by the patio each spring are a

Mother's Day gift from him and my daughter. The forsythia that brightens the side of the house, by the gate, he planted. The yellow and purple tulips and lilacs greet me from the beds he made for them. After it was over, every spade of dirt I turned, every bulb I planted, reminded me of him. Each time I put gas in the car, or set the table, he was missing.

But ultimately, more importantly, it was the overwhelming awareness that at least for me, the dreams of my life with a wonderful man, dreams that had begun long ago with those J. C. Penney catalog families, were never going to be, not because I was unlovable, but because I could never live this dream and still be me.

Now, after almost three decades of being single, it is impossible for me to make assumptions about what might have been had I stayed married or stayed with men who loved me. Certainly with Bob, I wouldn't have had to worry about mortgages or save up for extras but I might be waking up every morning bedeviled by the desire for a stiff drink or flirting darkly with schemes for ridding myself of his presence. I doubt we would have the warm, close relationship we now have, nurtured by our mutual love for our daughter and our sometimes tortured efforts to support one another as we respond to the pain we feel about her choices in life. With Kelsie, Tyler's father, I am certain that my life would have settled heavily into bleakness and emotional disarray. I write here as if I had a choice, and indeed, from the clear, quiet distance of almost thirty years, I did. However, in the turmoil of the moment, the suffocating weight of knowing I would tear lives apart and would hurt others in ways I could not predict was balanced by what I thought lay on the other side; peace, solitude, control of my days and nights, and the wide welcoming expanse of the unknown.

V
Doing it All

I went to Mexico for six months with a few books, two suitcases of clothes, most of which I set aside in favor of loose pants and cotton skirts, and a plan to write a book. I had never before had time defined as time for *me*; time to read and think and write without interruption. I had often done these things, but never without lacing them around the edges of necessity, or plugging them into the holes I found torn into the fabric of my day. Here I could wander to the square, *el jardin,* to watch the celebrations of San Miguel's birthday, stop for a coffee or a beer, or call an acquaintance to visit, but I could also stay on the patio in my pajamas, adding only a straw hat for protection from a sun that is stronger and closer than my Nevada sun, and read and write. My obligations fell away, replaced by an exhilarating feeling of being untethered, grounded only by my desire to find what I wanted to say, and how, and a new obligation to meet myself without the comfort of distraction and routine.

The long, rather tiresome debate about why women have not produced as much celebrated art or remarkable music as men is easily answered by simply looking at the time women have had to produce such things. The freedoms men have had to dream, to invent and to create have been far greater than those of women. Clearly, some women have overcome the limitations of children, husband and home and have done work that has changed the world. The feminists and suffragists Lucy Stone and Elizabeth Cady Stanton organized and wrote for women's rights after the children were in bed and in the predawn hours before they woke. Writers Louise Erdrich and Anne Lamott drew on the time they nursed their babies to write novels and essays that have spoken much-needed truths to many women. They have disentangled the complex ties of self and motherhood, and made them visible to women who share their experiences. But for the most part, unless they were very wealthy, women have never had time to do creative work of their own.

The relationships men and women have with work reveal that they occupy different worlds. The day for women is broken into unrelated, and sometimes conflicting, segments, pieces that fit together very poorly, if at all, often just falling into a jagged heap that is called a day, followed by night. Men are more likely to occupy a seamless expanse, focused on a narrow band of activity called work, leaving the rest of life's requirements up to someone else. Not only must a woman who feels driven to produce and create find the precious time to do her work, she must completely shift gears. Caring for a sick baby draws on a different level of a woman's resources than writing a paper or a chapter, a difference that both women and men minimize or ignore, erasing any validation for the impact that the strain between these two layers of life has on both mothering and work. An excerpt from my journal surprised me with the demands it describes, demands I took for granted, and my life was far more privileged than that of most women, single, with children, and working full time.

> *I woke at 7, slept very little. Kate was up with an earache most of the night. I took her to the pediatrician yesterday after my last class, but the penicillin has not yet worked. I finally took her into my bed about 3 and we both dozed. Today I will stay home with Kate because I have no classes, but tomorrow she has to be better so I can take her to the babysitter. Bob is out of town or he could take her for the day. Made oatmeal for both girls, Kate only ate a bit. They both love apple juice. I made a tuna fish sandwich for Tyler, almost out of mayonnaise, but will shop today if Katie is well enough. My car pool day so I bundled Kate up and took Tyler and the other kids to school. PTA meeting is tonight, but I won't go—missed last one too, but saw Tyler's teachers during Parent-Teacher conference and she is doing well except for some problem in math. She seems happy overall, quiet and self-contained. My paper for the Midwest meetings is due next Thursday and I have to finish the data analysis. Pat said she could stay with the girls while I'm away. Thank you, Pat.*

In the late 1970s I used the book, *Sociology for Pleasure*, by the sociologist Marcello Truzzi, in my classes at the University of Missouri in Kansas City. During that time, my daughters were about two and seven-years old, and I was either single or going through a divorce (these both being relatively frequent occupations of mine for about a decade). The acknowledgments section of his book summed up for me the vast discrepancy between the lives of men and women in the academy, and illustrated the different academic worlds we occupied, even as we shared the same space and the same expectations. In the acknowledgments he thanked his wife for her forbearance, maintaining the home and caring for the children while he spent long hours at his desk. He thanked his secretary for saving him the effort of having to leave his work and disturb his train of thought to get lunch, much less make it. This ritual of appreciation illustrates the taken for granted, unremarkable privilege of men and reveals the gaping distance between the productive realities of men and women. There was no wife at home caring for the children for me, no secretary to bring me lunch. Just a fact, not a request for sympathy, since I had chosen that profession, and I had chosen not to stay married. Yet, both Truzzi and I were trying to make it in the academy, and both of us were given tenure, promotions or merit increases based on the same standards of productivity and publishing, the only road which led to credibility as a scholar and a legitimate member of the academic community. How could anyone wonder why men are more productive? Or more to the point, why are women expected to adhere to standards that were not developed by them, that do not reflect their lives and responsibilities, given that they are the ones who almost always provide the essential, invisible, foundational work of mothering and making a home before they can move on to the next level—paid employment—the level where many men start? And more disturbing, why have so many women either not seen the discrepancy between their lives and that of their male peers, or just blindly committed themselves to overcoming all of the hurdles to meet the same standards?

For women, there is no one at home taking care of the children, preparing meals, doing the dishes, cleaning the house, taking the kids to school or the doctor, or doing the shopping. There is no wife to organize the birthday party, get supplies for school, buy new shoes, wash and iron the clothes, stay home with the sick baby, find a babysitter who will provide more than an assurance that the house won't burn down in your absence, take the car in for repairs or new tires, pay bills, give baths, read bedtime stories and tuck the kids into bed with love, sometimes with great sadness that the day has ended with so little time just for being there with them. I often put my girls to bed with my mind on the dishes that waited in the sink, the phone calls to be returned or letters to be written, or papers to be graded and lectures to be prepared for the next day. And I was far more fortunate than most women since I had such flexibility in my work and a dear friend, Patty, whose relationship to my children was close and enduring. Her love for my children was the love of a parent, responsible and nurturing and clear-headed. She helped with baths, dinner and homework, taking them shopping for clothes or to the zoo, replacing me whenever I could not be there.

Virginia Woolf was right; a woman needs a room of her own. But we also need the time to enter that room and do our work. Few women have ever had the pleasure of hours flowing seamlessly into one another in which to work and sleep and rest and play and work again. Days that fold imperceptibly into one another are foreign to most of us. Having not experienced the luxury of uninterrupted time, we can only guess at the enormous advantages this provides. We read about "multi-tasking" and how good we are at it, answering the phone with one hand, nursing the baby, supervising homework all at the same time—"I can bring home the bacon, fry it up in a pan . . ." And indeed women are, have had to be, more incorporative, more integrative, less linear than men. But if women could, for a month, or a year, live their lives as whole rather than segmented, if someone else did the laundry, took the kids to the dentist, made the meals and the beds, and cleaned the house, did all the invisible and time consuming work that women do, who knows what these unleashed women might do?

When I entered my Ph.D. program in 1970, it never occurred to me to see it as gendered in ways that left all women grappling with problems that men would never face. It was marvelously exhilarating just to be there, just to be one of the chosen, the few, as women pushed themselves into professions at the end of the 1960s. But the women's movement rapidly fueled the flames of feminist analysis and it wasn't long before we felt the heavy weight of the many male values, assumptions and privileges that dominated our experience and demanded adjustment from us if we were going to succeed. We needed to live up to expectations that men took for granted, to prove we were as smart, as analytical and intellectually tough as the men, while not putting them off by seeming too masculine.

To succeed in the academy meant that women had to play by men's rules, and we were so happy to get in it didn't occur to us, at first, that the deck was stacked against us. The doors opened, and even though they opened on a world in which men had the competitive advantage, we rushed in. We learned the ideas of male theorists from male professors and understood this to be scholarship, never questioning authorship, not wondering about the impact of gender on the theories we debated, not noticing the fact that men's lives were the only lives represented in our texts, not challenging the assumption that men were the only legitimate subjects of study and the only credible authors. Actually, at that point, consciousness for some of us was so embryonic that we couldn't imagine that there were any other theories or ideas of value, or that women's lives were worth studying. It wasn't just in the academy. Every other profession, except teaching and nursing, was, in the 1970s, a man's domain, and to succeed we needed to learn their language, and accept their assumptions and theories and facts. In every way, from the professors, to the material we studied, to the way the institution was structured, the academy was not just a man's world; it was *the* academic world.

For women in this world, achievement and academic success were to be added to the feminine, to "finish" us, make us more, but not in any way to challenge the definitions of femininity. To be feminine was still to be a little less than, not quite as smart, not as assertive or sure of ourselves, willing to be the "junior partner" rather than the senior, the second author rather than the first. We bought men's definitions of us for the most part, distancing ourselves from the wives of our fellow students at parties, shunning their discussion of children or cooking (not really knowing what they were talking about since we didn't actually talk to them), aligning ourselves with the men, following their conversations, contributing, but never overwhelming them.

Just because women were now admitted, even welcomed, didn't mean it wasn't still a man's world. The privileging of men in the classroom and in the core values of the institution was accompanied by sexual privilege. Sexual harassment laws were not yet in sight and sleeping with a professor was in many places more the norm than the exception; a choice that reflected a concern for the consequences of refusing as much as it arose from sexual desire. And as my friend, Maria, says, "it *was* the seventies" so having sex was pretty much like saying hello there for a while.

We were almost a model of hybrid femininity. Women graduate students were, it seemed, expected to create ourselves as a new type of woman, someone different than the women our professors and fellow students had married, but someone still desirable, feminine. On the one hand, we had as models "real women" who the men were married to, women who helped put them through school, had the babies and took care of the house, women whose lives reflected the expectations of the 1950s. These women might have looked like "earth mothers" or 'hippies" but were no different from their own moms in their shirtwaist dresses, taking their husbands to catch the train to the city, taking the kids to school and organizing barbecues in their backyards for the neighbors. The other models were women who had abandoned femininity for the male world, denied themselves husband and children, who had committed themselves to the profession and its demands, and had forfeited sex for professional success. The women who entered graduate or professional schools in the late 1960s and early 1970s were to forge a new path, celebrate their sexuality along with their scholarship, to package themselves as academic equals while preserving their essential femininity. They were to take themselves seriously but not so seriously as to challenge or offend the men who were their mentors. And, the femininity was a narrow one; the femininity of a girl, one who was learning and developing and becoming, rather than a solid and settled woman. The men might be married to women, but they wanted girls for colleagues.

I got pregnant with my first daughter while I was in graduate school. The chair of my program, the professor who had encouraged me to get a Ph.D., who helped me apply for fellowships and pushed me to succeed, was crestfallen. When I guiltily admitted my pregnancy, his disappointed response was: "How could this happen after all we have done for you?" Hurt at the time, I now see that he really did see two paths for women, productive scholar or wife and mother, not thinking that women would eventually want to change the way those paths had been cut. I immediately assured him that he "would never know I was pregnant," vowing to double my efforts to succeed, to "overcome" his concerns, to not disappoint him. My office mates, both men, agreed that if I wanted to get a Ph.D. I shouldn't have become pregnant, and they found no inconsistency between their response to me and the fact that one had a family with two children and the other's wife was pregnant with their first child. The reality that only women had babies did not seem to figure into their assessment of the situation. The anger and disappointment of my department chair, however, were not as hurtful as the outright hostility of one professor who must have seen my pregnancy as a violation of some sacred male space. I waited for over an hour for my final appointment with him at the end of the semester, leaving only when my labor pains became severe and frightening. He gave me an "incomplete" rather than a grade for the semester, justifying it by saying: "I thought you would just drop the kid and come back."

To my own permanent detriment, I completed my pregnancy without ever allowing myself to truly appreciate the experience, much less to celebrate it. I anticipated my baby's birth with only half of my heart, never fully committing myself, not crossing that line from scholar to mother, a line that separated two worlds I would always struggle to mesh, never living fully in one or the other.

When Mom, my father's mother, agreed to talk to me about her life, about her marriage and family and work, she protested that there wasn't anything interesting enough about it for anyone to want to know. Today I remember well the hours we spent talking and drinking ice tea thickened with sugar, the fan stirring the hot air, her little shapeless brown dog panting under her chair. She was reluctant to talk about herself and quietly skirted the uncomfortable areas, but what she did talk about revealed a life of hard work, few comforts and an acceptance of hardship and disappointment as natural and inevitable.

Like all farm wives of her generation, Mom spent her adult life just as she had spent her childhood: working. She and my grandfather had both grown up working, and their lives were built on the bedrock of the hard labor required for survival. She worked in the fields with her husband and children during planting and harvesting, and at mid-day, she cooked and served big dinners for the family and the field hands and cleaned up the kitchen while they rested on the porch before going back to the fields. She had a garden that fed the family all year. She and her daughters, Marie, Edna and Ila, and her son, Bob's wife, Sally, picked berries that grew by the road and apples and peaches from the neighbors' orchards. They canned all summer and into the fall, filling all of their cupboards and cellars. They killed and cleaned chickens, butchered hogs and salted the meat and hung the hams in the cellars to cure. They bought sides of beef from the butcher, and once had to buy another freezer to hold everything. She sewed all of the children's clothing, using the scraps for quilts. The quilt that covers my bed holds memories of the dresses my grandmother wore at the sink or in the garden, and the dresses my aunts wore to church or picnics.

When my own mother, a city girl, complained of the relentless farm work, Mom explained:

> *Every wife goes through that, Helen, wanting more, feeling burdened, but it isn't easy for the husband either. All that pressure to put food on the table, to not be a failure in his family's eyes. It wasn't easy for me or any of the kids.*

Mom wanted her children to escape the drudgery of farm life, and she was pleased that one daughter "married well" even if she didn't have any children, and that several of her sons had some financial success. James became an accountant in St.

Louis and John, my father, eventually gave up farming and, through real estate investments, gained the wealth he had long sought.

The thought of a space of her own never occurred to my grandmother, either as a child or as a wife and mother. Her identity was folded into that of the family, herself built on the demands of caring for seven children on a farm, a life of constant, exhausting work. Her later years were, for her, luxurious, freed from a lifetime of responsibility. She was able to carve out time for the deep and simple pleasures of friendships, reading and just being alone.

My grandfather, Willis, grew cotton and watermelons, fully aware of the forces of nature he could not overcome, bending to them when he had to, fighting them when he could. During the Depression, when his sons drove truckloads of watermelons to Nashville or Memphis, sometimes the bill for the transportation was larger than any profit they would have made. Pop gave President Roosevelt and his policies that allowed sharecroppers like him to buy their farms undying appreciation saying, "he give me that farm," his livelihood and identity for over thirty years.

Theirs was a life of obligation and responsibility, peppered only occasionally with the lightness of playing the fiddle or attending a social function. My father and his siblings experienced many of the same constraints their parents had, but the seven of them also played in the fields, and built small memories of games and fun that my grandparents never had. My grandmother's life was reflected in that of her daughter, Marie, who stayed in Advance, Missouri. She was the valedictorian of her high school, yet didn't go to college.

> *I know the girls was always resentful that we had the boys go to college and not them. Marie just hated that she had to work to help pay John's tuition, but it seemed like the girls was going to get married and the boys was going to have to support families, and it made the most sense for it to be that way. It worked pretty well, too. Bill didn't care much because he got that little store and married Pauline, and Bob never got more than beer under his belly, but the rest did okay. Marie was probably the smartest kid I had, but she married that no-good Clifford. I never could understand how she could stand that man. He come off the river boat just long enough to get her pregnant and left again, left her with thirteen children. No wonder she did such a good job when they hired her to work for Planned Parenthood. Marie rented a little place from us for a few years. She did most of the work and the kids helped when they was old enough. She was always so good to them kids. Seemed she lived her life for them, and never complained about nothing. Wanted them to go to college if they could, which is why she wanted them to go into the army.*

I remember visiting my mother's parents in St. Louis when I was five or six, from our farm in Tennessee, and later during our summer trips from Nevada to Missouri. I would spend as much time cleaning their apartment as my grandmother

Stewart would allow. Vacuuming the carpet, dusting the soft, wood tables and rearranging the magazines in their lovely apartment let me imagine I had these beautiful things and lived in that ordered, quiet place. My grandmother Stewart's life couldn't have been more different from Mom's, but at the base they both spent their lives devoted to family and children. Work on the farm or in the home was so demanding and so essential for the survival of the family for my grandmother White, and so necessary to maintain my Stewart grandparents' lifestyle, that a paying job was never a consideration. My grandmother Stewart didn't make her own soap or have a garden, but she managed money carefully and said, "if there was ever an extra dime, I sent the laundry out."

By the time my mother had five children, my parents lived on a chicken farm in Tennessee and my mother's days were filled not only with cooking and caring for children, but with making butter, pasteurizing milk, and feeding chickens, pigs and cows. She worked long hours in her garden, the dark soil gritty and stubborn under her nails. One year she and my father inoculated ten thousand baby chicks. And, although her work on the farm was absolutely essential, she was the "farm wife," and her long hours and hard work were seen as just a natural extension of my dad's paid employment, receiving no mention or reward.

My mother's parents sent them a subscription to *The New Yorker* every year for Christmas, symbolizing both the different worlds my parents came from, and the distance my parents wanted us to have from the dirt farms and small towns where we lived. My parents never assumed their children would *not* go to college. The years of working in the fields, picking grapes or apricots and digging potatoes, represented what we did, not who we were. We were always on our way up and out, away from where we were, moving ahead, living on the edge of the small towns where my father found jobs. Hard work was the only model we had, and that, coupled with the debates my parents had about politics and values that reflected their own disparate backgrounds, prepared us well for the educational path my parents had planned for us, all except my sister, who insisted from the time she was about twelve that she would leave home as soon as she was eighteen, and did. Holly spent the next twenty years traveling the world, living finally in Australia where her daughter and former husband still live. The rest of us learned the more mundane but valuable lesson of trudging ahead, of not being sidetracked or giving up, of not accepting defeat easily. Sometimes that meant closing our hearts to pain if we were humiliated, or if we failed, or if we were left or hurt by someone. This sometimes meant "doing" but not "being," whether it was marriage, teaching or maybe even mothering.

The hardships women faced in the 1970s and 1980s as they entered the labor force in droves were not new. Problems of discrimination in the workplace, unequal pay, sexual harassment, and the damaging economic consequences of divorce were commonplace, but now these injustices had names, they were identifiable to the hundreds and thousands of women who had accepted unfair treatment as simply the way things were. Women who worked could now challenge and denounce the expectations their mothers and grandmothers tolerated when they worked. The fact that discriminatory practices had been named was an indication that they were unacceptable, although not uncommon, and there were legal remedies that would have been unthinkable only decades earlier. The difficulties women identified revealed the growing importance of work and the separation of paid from unpaid labor. The types of obstacles that women of my generation were incensed about reflected the sweeping changes that had occurred in the span of just a few years. Women's demands for equal pay and other rights not only revealed the entrance of middle-class women into the workplace in large numbers, they also reflected a commitment to an identity that was not built only on motherhood and family. Only two generations earlier, women from middle-class families, like my mother's mother, were prohibited from working outside the home and their daughters were prepared only for becoming wives and mothers. On the other hand, poor women, like my grandmother White, had always worked, exempt from the powerful imagery of "true womanhood" that defined middle-class femininity. My grandmother, like other poor women, immigrant women, and black women who worked on farms, in factories and in other women's homes as domestic laborers only wanted relief from labor and hardship. These women endured low pay, long hours, sexual assaults, and often gave their paychecks to their fathers or husbands at the end of the week. The many conflicts tied to women's experiences with paid work in the 1960s and 1970s were built on these very different bases: a demand from middle class women to be let in, to participate fully, to be treated decently and compensated fairly, and the desire on the part of poor women to be able to opt out of work as they knew it, poorly paid, difficult and dispiriting.

The fatigue and isolation I felt as a mother and a worker were shared by untold numbers of women, probably all women who have children under less than perfect circumstances. My work, however, was constructed differently than work in the past. My work was different than the everyday, sometimes deadening weight of physical labor that was inextricable from the other demands met by rural women, farm women, those who did piece work in factories or at home. These were clearly not the women who demanded escape from the "problem that had no name," who saw work as an exciting diversion. These women found the goals of the women's movement absurd; they wanted a break from the demands of the world of work, rather than access to it. But those women who wanted to participate with men in work outside the home, whether because it would provide meaning to their lives or food on the table, once faced with the reality of the workplace, fought for and won protections that benefitted all working women. What may have begun as a desire on the part of educated, middle class women for more, for freedom from traditional definitions and opportunities, became rather quickly a desire to have basic rights in the work place. The women who wanted to work were also prepared to challenge the conditions they faced when their expectations were dashed, when they found themselves making less for doing more, when they were subjected to sexual innuendo and violence at work, and when they trained young *men* to succeed them in their positions. And, as the women's movement advanced, as men retreated from the confines of marriage and its attendant responsibilities, as the divorce rate increased and courts turned on women who wanted "equality" by taking their alimony and requiring their husbands to compensate them for a lifetime of child rearing and homemaking with only two years of "rehabilitative" pay, these women fought to change the harsh landscape at work and at home to reflect their needs and the needs of women at every class level. Middle class women might have ignored poor and minority women in their treatises and their organizations, but the battles they won were spread across the class terrain. It was middle-class women who had the resources and the connections and the leisure to raise issues like equal pay, freedom of choice and equal access that came to be identified with the women's movement, and who fought for them, benefitting all women through their efforts on their own behalf.

Ten years ago I was invited to give a talk on Mother's Day. I talked about the hypocrisy of setting aside one day to give flowers and cards to women who were as a class still getting paid much less than men, who were victims of battery and rape, and who were overly burdened by the conflicting responsibilities of raising children and trying to make a living. I condemned the ludicrous discrepancy between the idealization of motherhood and the everyday experience of motherhood. On a more recent Mother's Day, my daughter Tyler and I produced a beautiful brunch for my family, my mother, my brothers and their families, and several of my friends. Tyler stayed up until almost 4 a.m. making quiches and setting the table and cleaning the kitchen. That morning she woke early and produced a gorgeous display of fruit, ham, and quiche, set on starched white cloths among iris and mums and daisies. We wore light summer dresses, my mother wore a straw hat and a purple cotton skirt. Clusters of people settled on the deck or the patio, enjoying fresh coffee or wine spritzers. The bougainvillea stood against the pillars on the new deck, the hanging fuchsias were bright against the wicker beneath them as we celebrated this day, honoring our mother and all of the mothers there.

What has changed during these ten years? Very little. Women all over the world are still underpaid, overworked, and, in many countries, still bought and sold and totally dependent on men. They are still the victims of rape, beatings, stoning and other atrocities. In the Philippines and other countries, girls and women work for less than two dollars a day, making sports shoes and dresses to be sold in this country for hundreds of times that amount. The women in this country still suffer the inequalities they did ten years ago, but many of them no longer name their situation oppression, no longer condemn the patriarchy, no longer identify as feminist. Some of the women who protested so loudly twenty years ago are now in good jobs, happy with their own lives, and only peripherally in touch with the discrimination and burdens faced by increasing numbers of women and their children. Some of us who were so vocal twenty years ago have slipped into an acceptance of the things we cannot change, an awareness that if we are consumed with inequality, we have no time for the lives we have so carefully and with such sacrifices carved for ourselves. But hundreds of thousands of women still fight for women's equality, safety, for contraception, and an end to rape, violence and abuse in this country and globally. While all of these inequities persist, even as I condemn the pandemic of violence against women, against mothers, I can deeply appreciate what being a mother, one mother, has meant to me, and what I have given to my children through the years, and they, to me.

Work was not something I did. It was something I was. It stretched itself amoeba-like into all parts of every day, intermingled with the morning news and conversations at lunch, inseparable from what I had at one time thought of as the rest of my life. There was no "rest of my life." I realized at one point that nothing I did during the workday was counted by me as work; it was a meeting, or conference or teaching; something that interfered with work which was the production of a paper or article or lecture, and after picking up the children from school or day care and being the best mother I could be until their bedtime, I spent my evenings catching up on what I didn't do during the day. This definition condemned me to exhaustion. When Kate was a toddler, she woke one night thirsty and wet, and I carried her in my arms downstairs. I gained consciousness minutes later, broken glass on the floor, Kate standing over me crying hysterically. I lifted myself to sitting, then standing, and checked for damage I might have done to either of us. My doctor suggested a CAT scan and other tests to determine the problem, and they were all negative. I believe I just shorted out. We had all been sick off and on with the flu, and I had spent nights with little sleep. One night, changing Kate, I had found myself falling asleep at the changing table, sliding against the wall to the floor. I was young and healthy overall and I think that my body could absorb a great deal of neglect. But there were limits, which I had finally reached.

It has only been in the last two generations that we have lived like this, with the pressures to do everything, and to do it well—to succeed at meaningful work, and to provide our children a life that does not differ from that they would have if we were not gone from home for eight or more hours a day. Often we are alone, isolated in our own houses, solely responsible for our children's physical nurturing and their emotional development, and for providing a home, food and all the necessities. And while single fathers have long been applauded if they "do it all," single mothers have been criticized for trying to. When a man has custody of his children, the neighbors rally round, bringing casseroles, baking an extra dozen cookies, offering to have the kids overnight to give him a break. Single mothers in the same situation find themselves spread too thin, yet blaming ourselves for not being able to handle everything as well as we might. We mother in a world in which neither we nor others acknowledge the depth and expanse of the emotional and physical demands our mothering requires. While we earn a living, we also carve out the time and energy from our day to make meals, give baths and bedtime stories or later flute lessons and soccer practice, all as if this giant eight-hour chunk had not been removed from our day.

The choices I made about my work and my children drew me into situations I had not prepared for. I had never intended to raise my children alone, and yet on a daily basis, I could not imagine sharing them with anyone else. I had not planned to support myself and my children completely, but I became accustomed to the freedom I gained from having money. I had not thought a career was critical to me, yet, once having struggled to establish it, I could not let it go. I had not planned to get a divorce, yet rushed into divorce with great relief, not clearly aware of its finality. I saw divorce as a freedom, not feeling the cumulative pain of loss and failure until years later. I took my daughters from their fathers, not weighing the damage this would do to all of us.

Many of us care for our children on our own. If our great grandmothers were left to care for their children alone, it was seen as an aberration, a problem that needed to be solved through remarriage or the help of friends and family. On the frontier, sisters often stayed with one another after the birth of a child, or when the children were young, raising them if one sister died, even when there was a husband at home. In her book, *Private Faces/Public Places*, Abigail McCarthy writes about the isolating pain suffered by farm women on the plains who did not have this kind of family support. She paints a picture of the slow disintegration of the self women suffered when left alone, overburdened and underprepared. The isolation and hard work these women experienced is echoed today in the unspoken expectation that women can live and care for our children by ourselves, that we are inherently capable and efficient multi-taskers, able to juggle countless tasks and responsibilities without help or complaint. This equation of self-sufficiency with self-worth creates hardships for all of us. Charlotte Perkins Gilman, the feminist economist, wrote at the turn of the twentieth century about the need for an alternative for women so they could share cooking, cleaning, and childcare to make time for a creative life. Her novel, *The Yellow Wallpaper*, is heavy with the despair felt by and the damage done to a woman whose depression after the birth of her baby resulted in her doctor's decision that her recovery depended on isolation and quiet, a cure that drove her insane.

I believe, in part, that women, during the decades of the sixties, seventies and eighties incorporated the dominant cultural disavowal of the importance of motherhood, even as we were increasingly expected to mother alone and with little support either in the community or at work. Our protestations that biology wasn't destiny, that women weren't biologically determined to be mothers or nurturers or emotional and irrational, necessary perhaps to overcome the deep-seated biases against women which painted them as intellectually and professionally inferior, led to our own acceptance of the cultural devaluation of our roles as mothers. We lived in a culture in which mothering was defined as natural and instinctive and we accepted the view that our mothering simply reflected our sex, even as we rejected the notion that we should be defined in terms of that natural ability—we were more than that.

We were actually caught in a rather powerful trap. If mothering was a natural, instinctive impulse, then it obviously didn't take much effort or intelligence and shouldn't be rewarded substantially, even though we were still expected to devote our time and energy to it and to build our identity on how well we mothered. On the other hand, if mothering was natural and innate for women, to not completely devote oneself to mothering and abandon it for work or school or to not do it well or easily was to risk being seen as a social deviant—not only was she not a good mother, she was not a good woman.

One potential consequence of the devaluation of "mothering" and the parallel rejection of "woman as natural mother" was that the significant discrepancies in the economic positions of men and women could easily result in men being much more able to meet the criterion of "most able to provide" for the child in the new "no-fault divorce" system. How could women, who were paid less than men and who struggled at work under the new rules, partly because of their children, justify custody of their children or any special relationship with them if they were claiming that they weren't distinct from men because of their mothering instincts, a particularly vexing problem since no-fault divorces were rapidly gaining in popularity in state after state?

Because mothering was considered a natural impulse, the work we did at home was, while necessary, viewed as insignificant and not deserving of any special notice or compensation, either from ourselves or from anyone else—it was simply not real work. The only real work was work outside the home. When I was in junior high school my mother got a job as a hostess at Uncle John's Pancake House in Reno and we thought she was a minor celebrity, dressed up, made up, hair done up, leaving the house every day. Once in a while my dad would take us there for breakfast and we basked in our special relationship to the woman who seated us at the booth and brought us our menus and water. This was her first "real job." She was not nearly as pleased to have it as we thought she should be.

Not only did we define away the value of mothering, much of what we did every day was not considered work. We spent enormous amounts of time and expended great energy doing heavy physical and emotional labor that was basically invisible, taken for granted and certainly unpaid. Work was what one got paid to do, so men worked, women did everything else required for survival and if they didn't do it well, didn't keep the kids in clean clothes and the house in order, and make nourishing meals three times a day, they were judged as slovenly and lazy and their husbands were pitied. My friend, sociologist, Elaine Enarson, provided a wonderful example of the definition of work, which reveals how women's work is diminished; imagine a traditional family going on a picnic at the beach, an activity most define not as work but as leisure. The mother buys the supplies, packs the lunch, gathers up the bathing suits, towels, extra clothes, extra diapers, sun screen, and makes sure everyone has shoes and jackets in case the weather changes. The father fills the gas tank and drives to the beach where they all unload the car, carrying the umbrellas, blankets, towels and picnic supplies to a sandy spot near the water. The mother, after slathering the kids with sunscreen, unpacking the picnic, distributing the sandwiches and chips and melon, then demanding that the children wait a half hour before swimming, perches tensely on the sand counting heads until time to pack up and go home. She unpacks and put things away, bathes the kids, gets them in bed, and washes the towels, bathing suits and clothes and cleans the sand off of everything. Not a moment of real work. Women are to spend their lives doing things that are unrecognized in the doing, but critical in their absence.

Though it may offer some financial relief, marriage today has not removed the expectation that women take responsibility for their husband, their children, their house. Even when the woman works full time, she still does most of the childcare and housework. It is true that the man's participation has changed, but relatively little, and he still "helps out" and "baby sits" rather than taking full responsibility. This is so universally expected that it is difficult to make a legitimate claim that it should be done differently. I knew that if I had stayed married to Kate's father, I would have been the one getting up and changing the diapers and getting the juice, and getting breakfast in the morning before I went to work, and buying groceries and making dinner after. I would have probably had the same fatigue I experienced as a single mother, only it would have been laced with bitterness and hostility because I would have felt unloved and uncared for in my marriage. I could handle feeling unloved and uncared for, just not by a man to whom I was married.

When I teach about women and work, I unfailingly hit an impenetrable wall that runs parallel to the contradictions I feel about Mother's Day. We are enmeshed in subtle and unspoken conflicts between opportunities and constraints. We succeed in ways we might not have anticipated yet struggle with deep prejudices that are so taken for granted as to be invisible. It is dishonest and destructive to assert that women now have equal access and equal opportunity in the university, or any other institution for that matter. True, we are not legally excluded, nor do we face quotas. Yes, we are accepted into graduate school and are taken seriously—the chilly climate has warmed in the last decade or so. But the rules we must follow, the manner of our participation remain different from those men follow. It may be that they are happily oblivious to their privilege, or more likely, they want to remain consciously oblivious because to know and to see would require that they support changes if they are to retain their sense of selves as educated, egalitarian men. The consequences of awareness are dramatic. For men to acknowledge that women have to adjust to male rules and male definitions, to manipulate their lives to fit man-made institutions, forces them into an uncomfortable and largely unwelcome re-analysis of themselves. They have too much to lose to change easily. And neither women nor men want to impose guilt on men, guilt that leads to resentment and avoidance. So women have the difficult job of participating in a world which is not designed for our lives, for the reality that we bear children and nurture them and undertake the social and emotional responsibilities for our families in addition to providing economically and valuing ourselves and being evaluated in terms of what we produce in the world of work. In addition, if we want to have a relationship with a man, we have the delicate task of living with significant disadvantages without becoming bitter or accusatory. And indeed it is not only necessary to travel this path carefully to maintain a loving relationship with a man, it is necessary if one is to live fully, an endeavor which demands the acknowledgment of constraints without feeling imprisoned, working out a full life within a system which invisibly constricts.

Women can acknowledge the gender-based problems we experience in the world we share with men and still maintain a vision of the world which includes these relationships. This is not to say that we don't feel anger or frustration, that we don't realize that the demands we face at work are more difficult than those faced by men, but it means that we are not overwhelmed by these feelings, or more accurately, because sometimes we may be overwhelmed, we are not destroyed by them, nor do we destroy others. Is this giving up? Is this selling out? I know I would have thought this in the past. I know I could not have been accepting of these contradictions and I would have seen the acceptance of such struggles as capitulation. We absorb the contradictions we live with and they can be either devastating or nourishing, sometimes they are both at different times. Just as we can enjoy the simple pleasure of a glass of wine knowing full well that AIDS and genocides are devastating millions of people in Africa, we love the men in our lives knowing they have privileges we don't or we turn our knowledge about inequity or oppression into action against it while not being defeated by its scale and expanse.

Clearly, the work my grandmothers and my mother did raising their children, farming, and keeping house, could be exhausting, seemingly endless, and all-consuming but no more so than the work done by the women who raised other people's children and scrubbed their floors before going home to their own hungry children and dirty dishes, and that, only if they were lucky. Today, many women are still doing that kind of work, but many more now combine mothering and the responsibilities of home with work in large institutions, bureaucracies like hospitals, brokerage firms, social service agencies, banks, law offices, and universities, a kind of work that many of us expected to be personally and economically fulfilling and in which we had demanded to be included. We often see these institutions as built for men, by men, with male values and privileges, but we may not see as clearly that these institutions also prove inconsistent with women's values and emotional lives. I have worked in a university for over thirty years, and know the enormous benefits and subtle and eroding costs of this kind of work. Despite the fact that the work we do in these institutions does not break our backs like working in the fields or factories, despite the lack of physical hardship and demands on our bodies, noise, rudeness, lack of respect and generally oppressive working conditions, the destructive pressure of these vast bureaucratic institutions can be emotionally deadening. Our work, at least my work, seems built on the premise that we live in neutral, never shifting into high or low gear. There is no room for exuberance in most institutional settings, the ceilings and floors converge, narrowing our range of expression to its most mundane and predictable. My colleagues have a book published and they casually mention it; they are "pleased." Or, they are refused promotion and the impact of the decision disappears behind their office door. The academy is a flat land, at best one of gently rolling hills, the seasons remain the same—the sun never blinding, no strangling winds, no harsh winters. The self can shrivel in this bleak, numbing sameness. The spirit yearns for some rough waves, some burning sand, some steep precipice, something against which to battle, something to overcome or to celebrate.

The self most acceptable to the vast institutions in which we live so much of our lives is mild, not gentle really, but tepid, half responsive, rather than fully responsive. The wildness of our sexual passion, the terrifying love we have for our children, the depth of pain we feel at loss or abandonment are smoothed from our physical and emotional selves as we move through our lives there. This sense of rounding off, of polishing any rough edges, of cautiously selecting words and re-framing every major battle as a skirmish of no personal significance erodes the self, leaves it uncommitted and flaccid. The power accompanying anger, the clarity that follows pain, are lost in this world of mid-range feelings, dulled by demands for reasonableness and caution. And yet, success in these institutions demands this deadening. Deadening may be too strong a word, perhaps denial of women's spirit, the range of emotion we are encouraged to have in every other area of our lives, the emotions we know from our close connection with our children and our lovers.

I have often had conflicts about this, wanting to reject the institutional demand for sobriety and placidity, yet I have depended on acceptance in this monotonic world. I have been dispirited by the calm and the expectation that expression should be limited to verbal or written analysis, eschewing emotion. In my work I have often felt myself to be too much—too tall, too loud, too smart, too stupid, too awkward, too imposing, too attractive, too ugly. Alternately, I have felt raw and exposed, then hidden and cowering. There was no comfortable way to have the range of life I wanted and to be in that hushed world. Being quiet is not the same as being hushed. Quiet is opening, spacious, allowing huge movements and daring. Hushed is repressed, closed and thwarted. The academic world is hushed.

I taught at the same university from the time I was in my late twenties until I was almost forty-five. It seems unreasonable that only fifteen or sixteen years could transport me from youth to middle age. The next ten years did not age me nearly as much. I struggled mightily during that time with the pull of my academic self against what I saw as my spirit, my soul that went un-nurtured, and became flattened rather than robust and rich. The limitations on expression were not formalized of course, but the daily social world demanded not simply civility, which seems to be a necessary acceptance and acknowledgment of another, but emptiness and distancing from oneself and what one produced to the point of emotional disengagement. One spring, a very well known, highly respected sociologist came to the University to give a series of lectures and as several of us were driving with him to lunch, he remarked on the stupidity and wastefulness displayed by a couple of young people who were running in the fresh sunshine. This was a man who had never married, who lived in an apartment right on the campus where he taught, and whose life was almost completely devoid of social or physical activity. This was the model for the successful sociologist. This was a life that seemed to me dreadfully limited, distasteful, and empty. Daily I felt the pressure to publish, to produce, to actually, as the chair of my Ph.D. program used to say, *be* a good product. Yet, I lived a completely different life with my daughters, soaked in their lightness and laughter, occupied by their homework and their own busy lives, their warmth and needs. To navigate these conflicts demands a strong sense of self, one not completely given over to some professional identity, and for me this was very hard. I had given so much of myself to the idea that I would be successful, had left two marriages determined to raise my children on my own, plowed through the unrelenting demands of doing it all, pushed by the ideology of the nascent women's movement, succumbing to its mandates, and left exhausted and brittle by my efforts.

One summer, when my daughters and I were traveling from Kansas City to San Francisco by train, we came through a tiny town, somewhere in Kansas, about ten o'clock at night. During the few minutes we were stopped there, letting sleepy passengers off and a couple of families on, I almost gathered up the girls and got off. I imagined getting a job in a café where I would work an eight-hour shift, Tyler would go to the small elementary school and I would find a nice older woman in the neighborhood to watch Kate. The simplicity, the quiet and the depth seemed so restful and real. I have never forgotten that small town. There was another town, this time one we drove through on a trip from Nevada to Missouri. I don't remember what state it was in, Kansas maybe, but it had the feel of a small town in the south; huge trees, their roots heaving the sidewalks, a park cooled by deep groves of trees, winding paths, a carousel from the twenties or thirties in the center. Narrow two story houses rested on graceful lawns, small shops offered books and clothing, a movie theater on the main street, the marquis ornate with faces and flowers and vines, announced a second run movie. But I didn't stop there either. I had made commitments, and just as I had gone to Kearney, Nebraska from Colorado when I was a young mother because I had signed a contract, though the situation was so uncomfortable for me that all I could think of was how to leave, I continued on to Kansas City. I had a job; Tyler was to start college in the fall, and I didn't have the courage to give up the security I had and the world I knew for something completely different. But I remember the sensation of walking down those broken sidewalks in the late afternoon, feeling as if I had grown up there and had walked down those welcoming streets with my brothers and sister every summer day.

VI
Coming Undone

I hadn't planned to mother alone, to be completely responsible for two daughters, to move far from my family and take a job in a city where I knew no one, yet I had made these choices, and I had made these choices without truly considering how they would actually play out in the long term. I met the consequences with what I knew; hard work, commitment, overcoming and achievement, responses that left me utterly unfulfilled. Most people saw a smiling, competent, accomplished and strong young woman. They saw a woman who was loving and warm. They did not know she was also frequently joyless, or that she often despised herself. What they saw was not a lie; but it was the other part, an equally real part, the entire outer casing which held this core of ugliness and worthlessness. This box, this shell, was thickly padded with success and activity and a disarming wit. It denied the reality of the soft, rotten center. But it was always there, and I could always dip down into it, grab the sludge and fashion a wretched shroud for myself. Fear and anger periodically tore through the mask of composed calm, colliding with the public face, leaving a wide path strewn with remorse and guilt on my part, unanchored guilt and fear on the part of my daughters.

I believe much of the torment of those years of depression was unavoidable. I think it had very little to do with my childhood, my parents, my early years, although it is undeniable that depression and addiction have woven rough threads through the fabric of my family for several generations. The genetic connection to depression and addiction may have shaped the demons into particular forms, but it did not create them. My father was often joyless and melancholy, as was his father. He drank too much and too carelessly as a young man and, by the time he was an adult, had a real problem with alcohol. One of his brothers spent all of his adult life teetering on the edge of alcoholism. My brothers admit to a cautious suspicion of alcohol, and one gave up drinking decades ago. My sister surrendered to the devastations of alcoholism early on, letting it own her during much of her life, although today her commitment to her art has sent any reliance on alcohol to the edges of her life. One of my daughters has struggled with severe depression for twenty years and the other with drugs and alcohol for over a decade. My mother is the one woman in our family who seems truly free of the river of depression in which some of us have spent so many years. It may seem that I am suggesting lives that form a mosaic of emotional wreckage, but that is too encompassing, too bleak and weighty. Rather, alcoholism and depression insidiously lodged themselves in the corners and under the furniture of our lives, opportunistically binding themselves to us when we were not watching.

Depression was not my only emotion, but it was a powerful, enveloping heaviness that flowed threateningly around my everyday movements, lying in wait for the right moment to strike, half-submerged in a dark pool from which it would rise to pull me under, almost drowning me before releasing its grip again. Sandwiched between the venomous phone calls from Kelsie, the absolute physical collapse with the divorce from Bob, the loss of Geoff and the disgust I sometimes felt for myself after classes or presentations, I had respites of happiness that I knew were fleeting, and the contentment I felt made me vulnerable and afraid. I felt an almost consuming adoration for my children, their softness, their potential, the magic of their precious beings. A walk in Loose Park in Kansas City on a soft evening, or running though my neighborhood just as a rainstorm erupted, wrapped me in awe and wonder, while not erasing the threat of imminent despair.

It may well be that I would have suffered depression for almost two decades in my thirties and forties even if I had lived a life of complete irresponsibility and privilege. Maybe if I had remained married to a loving and kind husband, had I found one, and had children with no needs or demands of their own, and had not tried to achieve in a stressful career, I still would have become as confused, self-loathing and hopeless as I did. Maybe the depression, the black numbness, was completely chemical and would have enveloped me in any case. Maybe, in fact, seeing that I interpreted the "life of the mind" in academia as stultifying and stagnant, the placidity and smooth simplicity of the suburbs would have been even more emotionally and mentally poisonous. Nevertheless, the combination of physical exhaustion I felt as a result of being a single mother and trying to succeed in my work, and the demands I made on myself to be a perfect parent, friend, and scholar eroded the foundation of my identity. My blind, unexamined commitment not to reveal weakness or neediness shaped my response to the pressures I felt. In part, having reaped the benefits of the women's movement, having choices my mother and grandmothers did not have and having made choices within the context of that freedom, I was unwilling to see the deep contradictions I was living with.

I probably began early on to imperceptibly and unconsciously steel myself against those contradictions. I had entered graduate school aware of the pull between having a man I wanted and having a Ph.D., but unaware of the depth and power of the conflicts this would produce, blithely assuming it could all be done smoothly with only a bit of effort on my part. Even after Kelsie and I were divorced, I was convinced that our divorce was the result of his insensitivity and selfishness, and that all the pieces of the life I wanted could be meshed with another partner. And that *can* happen. People do walk these difficult tightropes with relative ease every day. But, for me, the relentless drive to achieve, the investment of my self-worth in my ability to handle everything well and even admirably, came up against the overwhelming demands I felt and led me to harden myself against any loosening of expectations I held for myself. Rather than see that I was overwhelmed, I saw that I needed to work harder to handle the responsibilities I had. I was a sociologist, steeped in an analysis of structural problems rather than trained to see problems as individually initiated, and though I knew there were implicit problems facing any of us who thought we could live the dreams we held onto from childhood and the dreams inspired by the freedom and choice we later gained, I turned my energies to simply doing more and doing it better.

The need I felt to build a perfect family despite the obvious lack of the main player, the father, may have been situated in the clichéd desire to give my daughters what my childhood hadn't offered. But even more important to me was the desire not to succumb to the stereotypes about the impact of divorce on children—that the mothers couldn't give their kids the attention and parenting they deserved, that their children didn't participate in plays and soccer like other children, or rather, if they did, the mother was too busy at work to come to rehearsals or bring oranges or snacks to the games, that the home was in disarray and everyone ate on the run. This required not just overcoming the physical and emotional hurdles every single parent faces, but convincing others I was doing that competently.

I tried to balance impossible conflicts, for example to be a single parent yet to make sure my girls had a dad in their life; to recognize the stupidity and damaging bureaucracy of the public school system and yet have my daughters succeed in it. Kate's father's blithe comments about the "pathology of the single mother home" underscored all the negative assumptions about my family, effectively challenging all of my efforts and my assertions about its adequacy, spurring me to do more. My children would be successful academically, would be on the swim team, in the school plays, and I would be there for every PTA meeting, swim meet, soccer game and opening night. I worked to construct a world that was protected, warm, bright and open, making space for my daughters and me to play and work with energy and joy. My children and their friends ran up and down stairs, out to play, in for lunch, playing games, reading stories, riding bikes, coming and going from one house to another in our neighborhood. Screen porches provided cool shelters for playing dolls and Pretty Pony in the summer. Sunny rooms took their place when the weather turned cold. Neighborhood children and friends' children, neighborhood plays, sleepovers indoors or in tents, trips to the zoo, outdoor theater, aunts and uncles and cousins all nourished the childhood of my daughters. But all this effort to create an idyllic childhood that belied the assumptions about divorced professional women came at a heavy cost. My daughters were under enormous pressure to hold up their end of the bargain—I was counting on them to make me a good mother.

I treated my daughters' childhoods in some ways as a storage shed for memories. Just as I saved their dresses and shoes, dolls, birthday cards, wrapping paper and ribbons, I wanted to save their experiences for their future. It was almost as important to provide these memories as it was for them to experience the event, so Thanksgivings and Christmases and birthdays and every other moment that could be celebrated was produced by me for them. Not surprisingly, such an approach to being a parent left lots of room for imperfection. I needed to create the perfect world to convince myself that I was a good mother, that being a single mother would not sling me into the mud of neglect, dependence, and inferiority that I feared. The family I fashioned so carefully consisted of an accomplished, loving, competent mother, talented and intelligent daughters, beautiful alone or framed together, looking much like the families I had cut from the Sears catalog when I was a child. The efforts to provide wonderful holidays, the most memorable graduation or sixteenth birthday, the prettiest dresses and cutest bonnets for the Easter egg hunts, fun and nutritious lunches wrapped in pretty paper, were all part of that picture. I wanted these moments to conform to the hazy images of perfection that had been portrayed in every magazine I had read and every movie I had seen.

The foundational structures of my world were carefully constructed, mostly of responsibility, and the demands were delicately laced together, interwoven in a complex relationship of interdependence. Sometimes the most inconsequential event would cut through the veil between the self and the mask of competence and calm I had so carefully constructed. This happened one Easter morning, when Tyler was about seven and Kate was about two. Easter in Kansas City is a big, happy celebration; a parade on the Plaza, huge plaster bunnies decorated with bonnets and baskets. I had bought both of the girls lovely, special dresses—new socks, new shoes and hats for Easter. I had arranged pretty baskets, with that slick, plastic grass, candy eggs and little stuffed chicks and ducks. I had colored eggs and hidden them in the yard. We went to church, because it was Easter, and the music was especially beautiful on that Sunday. On the way home, all of us in our spring dresses, having constructed the ritual of Easter just as it was supposed to be, the girls argued about an Easter egg or something equally unimportant, and I came undone. Not that this firestorm came very often, but holding it in abeyance took effort, and when it descended upon us, it raged out of control.

We could all forget, did forget, for long periods of time that the exterior walls embracing our lives were so fragile that when one strong reed was severed from the others it could tear them apart, ripping through them, shredding the fine light ribs that made the structure whole, unraveling and escalating, until the fragile fabric collapsed onto itself. When the worlds I was trying to hold up collided or when one bled into another, I was swiftly and completely undone. When this delicate structure was jolted it was likely to fall, and when it did, I was overcome by frustration and self-loathing and lashed out at everything; the children, the house, myself. When the anger dissipated, it left me empty and as fragile as a crystal glass. My world was so brittle, tied together by such thin threads, and spun so tightly, that when one tiny thread began to unravel, the entire structure of my life could be destroyed in a moment. Today, when my daughter, Tyler, struggles with depression, trying to beat away the persistent voices of inadequacy and worthlessness, I think the only memory she has salvaged from her childhood is the guilt and fear she felt at my anger.

The depression that overtook me was visceral. It felt like ice-skating slowly on a thick, porous lake of paraffin, like that my mother put on the top of jars of jam and jelly, or being abandoned on a frozen slab in the middle of a dreary and uncivil land. The recurrent half-waking, half-sleeping envelope of sensation was of a gray, empty expanse, opaque and fuzzy but very dense, immovable, locked in by heavy damp air. The years of bondage to depression and its aftermath I share with millions of people. I knew full well the anger and depression I felt so frequently for so long weren't normal. But I felt absolutely consumed by them, completely out of control, desperate, my entire world emptied of meaning, convinced that nothing of value could be regained.

The line between depression and anger and self-hatred has sometimes been imperceptible in my life. For many years, especially those years when my children were young, anger was the powerful, threatening animal sulking in a corner of my soul. Later, I was stalked by emptiness and self-doubt and feelings of worthlessness, and more recently, a heavy sense of meaningless and powerlessness which wrapped me tightly in emotional isolation. After the anger, drained and guilty, I was weak and confused by the dark power of rage. I railed at my weakness, my selfishness and my destructiveness. I condemned myself for being self-centered, for not appreciating my gifts, for not appreciating my healthy and clever children, a lovely house, good car and job and friends. What was this evil, this ugliness that overcame me?

And when I slowly regained myself after the slashing self-abuse I knew that I had been completely unreasonable. But that didn't mean I understood where this loyal misery originated or how to rid myself of it.

In response to these feelings of inadequacy or inauthenticity, I increasingly began to retreat, to steel myself to walk through a minefield of contradictions and conflicts. It is clear that the way I responded to these feelings of hollowness and despair reflected what I had learned so well—that my value came through hard work, overcoming, achievement and success. These were the values that had worked well for my brothers and me, and yet, were now leading to a sense of isolation and self-loathing that I couldn't understand.

I began to feel that my colleagues and I were all contributing insignificant and relatively meaningless articles or papers on obscure or abundantly obvious issues to other sociologists who found them useful primarily as references for their own equally uninteresting work. Actually, now that I think about it, that is how a lot of people still feel about sociology. I denigrated my colleagues who typified the deep condemnation I felt for myself. At professional meetings, the academics were recognizable in even the largest hotel among hundreds of other guests by their dress and demeanor, a studied stylistic blandness and physical slovenliness that signaled intellectualism. I could not guarantee that one could differentiate sociologists from psychologists or anthropologists or perhaps any number of other disciplinary adherents, but we could easily be distinguished from anyone outside the academy. The men had carelessly rumpled themselves together in "high water" corduroy pants, a beige or brown sweater or jacket hanging on their flimsy frames, face camouflaged behind a sparse, pubic beard. The women were draped in shapeless cotton, wearing bulky sandals with socks, their hair hanging lank, or gelled into aggressive tufts. Together they wandered the conference rooms and hallways, stocking up on whatever free buffet items might be available, and spending obligatory time as members of a bored, yet smugly critical audience. They waited for the question and answer period so that they might find some statistical or methodological flaw that would render the speaker's points meaningless, or so that they might hitch their own research endeavors to one of those speaker's contributions. This image, neither positive nor nurturing, was born of my sense of disconnection from myself and from my work, and has been largely abandoned along with my depression.

The difficulty I had connecting with my profession had more than one source. The lifelessness and flatness of academia, the discounting of exuberance, was one part of the problem. The other had to do more with my separation from myself. While I was able to go through the motions that would convince others that I was engaged and credible, my performance was so split from my feelings about it and myself that the predictable outcome was self-derision, contempt or self-hatred. Yet, there was no retreat; the very solidly grounded script of working hard, overcoming and succeeding kept me pushing ahead, preparing, presenting and publishing.

When I was a member of a panel discussing "the Mommy track" which I felt very competent to discuss, both at a personal and a professional level, I recall making good points, arguing them well and backing them up with other resources. When I was finished, it was as if I hadn't been there at all, but had produced words and thoughts that were meaningless and insipid. I walked home from the University that afternoon wrapped in emptiness. I was owned by a sense of not being real, of having done something as a different person, of being completely separate from the person I was in that lecture hall, and, what is worse, I despised myself. I was a hulking shell with nothing to contribute, vacant, useless, and valueless. No matter how well qualified, no matter how good my lecture or presentation, I left the room loathing my words, my gestures and myself, wanting only to escape and erase the experience, to reach down into some small comforting part of myself and pull it around me until I could again face myself and others. There were so many days, from the first year at the University, that I walked to my classes after hours of preparation, dreading the time with my students, accusing myself of every stupidity and intellectual failing as I spoke, the only positive feeling upon leaving being that it was finally over. Something as forgivable as a mispronounced word caused days of agonized self-doubt and humiliation. I could easily dismiss the positive evaluations of others, but I remained hyper-vigilant to the negative evaluations, for the critics' condemnations, suffering painfully in a process that resulted in a devastating erosion of the self.

This enormously painful and destructive process went on for years, and after each wrenching self-exposure and subsequent self-condemnation, I would determine to do it again, do it better, do it more, do it differently. Since I never perceived any improvement in my work, always finding some previously hidden flaw, my professional life was agonizing at times. At the same time, I had a great deal of interest in my field, and I wanted to share what I knew, to talk with others, to teach and to present. Objectively, I was articulate in my presentation and was producing interesting work, but no amount of objective evaluation could compensate for the wretchedness of my self-judgments. Publishing was slightly better than teaching and lecturing because the face-to-face interaction could be avoided. In either case, if I wanted to succeed, I needed to forge on, regrouping after each failure to brace for another.

Depression is not all bad of course. It has much to recommend it in hindsight. The struggle provides an opportunity to know oneself at one's worst which perhaps serves as a foundation for self-awareness, and change (not that I would recommend it as a growth experience) but while it takes residence in your soul, it is an insidious, vicious enemy.

I was loath to accept an anti-depressant as the answer. I certainly got my babies their inoculations and all their boosters, and I relied on prescription medications for ear infections and yeast infections, and I knew I had to take my thyroid medication every day or my body would eventually nosedive. But a pill to fix my malaise, my melancholy, my sporadic bouts of self- hatred and annihilating anger was, I thought, an unreasonably simplistic intervention on the complex self.

My doctor prescribed Prozac as easily as if he were prescribing an antibiotic or telling me to gargle. I was not completely comfortable with mind-altering drugs other than those we had used in the sixties, and I considered that I might just be self-indulgent, weak, or faddish. But, I was in the middle of middle age and I was tired of living with the destructive force of depression.

As the depression lifted, I became more at ease overall. I was no longer so dark beneath my surface, and I didn't have to struggle to avoid the eager grasp of self-deprecation. There was a freedom of movement, both physical and intellectual that I had not felt for any sustained period for so long. Perhaps the overwhelming feeling I had is that I felt like "myself." This description, I now know, of feeling like oneself is commonly offered by people who take Prozac. I puzzle over "feeling like myself" because it implies that there is a self somewhere internal that is not allowed expression until released by this medication. This would mean, then, that the feelings of despair or hollowness or fear are not authentic or genuine parts of the self, but are encroachments on the self. I'm not really clear about the relationship between a drug and "the self," but I continue to benefit from the effects of Prozac

My oldest daughter is a wonderful actress, a creative writer, a thoroughly unusual and delightful person whose mind explores the crevices and heights of life's landscape rather than its plains. She is quick and witty and completely unpredictable. She has also sometimes despised herself so much that she could not leave the house for fear that her mere presence would frighten others. For years, Tyler was overwhelmed by self-hatred and the feeling that she was never good enough, wealthy enough, pretty enough or thin enough, and on and on. She fantasized horrible things, saw vicious monsters at her window and door, slashed herself, threw up when she ate, was afraid of going outside, afraid that her ugliness would hurt other people. She tried so hard to fight her depression; she took hot showers, dressed carefully, and determined to be happy.

Even if I had created perfect memories of an idyllic childhood, I could not have made up for the most profound loss in my older daughter's life; the loss of her father. I could not fill the hole my daughter kept trying to fill. I had taken her from him, refusing his judgments of me, leaving the bitterness, isolation and distance for the comfort of solitude. I left him because I couldn't give up a future I had worked for, with sometimes painful commitment, for a future which promised to defeat any feelings of intellectual adequacy or personal worth I had achieved. With Kelsie, I could look forward to debilitating conflict and icy recriminations. After I left him, what had been selfishness and pride on his part gathered itself into hatred and malice, and he hurled vicious torrents of blame at both Tyler and me for years.

For this daughter, every gift, every effort, every ordinary mother's commitment to provide the best opportunity and the most fulfilled childhood was accepted with reservation. The acceptance was tinged with disappointment that it could not have been more, or better, or sometimes, just different. The rejection by her father, which bred her rejection of herself, diminished her value, and was mirrored in her conviction that everything that came to her was damaged because she was damaged. She yearned for her father who would sometimes tell her he loved her and should have her with him, the same father who also spewed sexual accusations and sickening vitriol on her. After she talked to him, or saw him, she often vomited, lay depleted on the couch or her bed, sometimes for days, aching with grief for not being a daughter he could love, for being so despicable that even her own father could not embrace her.

For weeks, sometimes months, she was fine, but then would become suddenly enveloped by blackness. She was physically sick, nauseated, achy and weak. She was listless and heavy spirited for days and then weeks. I was usually patient; sometimes, however, I just couldn't believe she couldn't do better on her own, feel better. She was young, beautiful, educated and had loving family and friends. She was talented, had a good sense of humor. What right did she have to be full of self-hatred, how dare she despise herself, my daughter, be afraid to have people see her lovely face because they would think she was a monster and run from her?

During those years, she was hospitalized several times and saw therapists of every stripe. She tried every medication she was offered, depending on the diagnosis. The diagnoses were tossed around as if they didn't devastate us each time. The prognoses were offered with a casualness that belied the predictions of a future plagued by mental illness. Some therapists blamed alcoholism in the family and others blamed me. They always wanted to meet with the family, talk about childhood, about family history. Even though I felt blamed, angry, and defensive, I needed them to help her. I didn't believe them, thought their diagnoses were trite and false and faddish. Yet, I depended on them. I hated the twenty-eight day insurance-driven programs, the pat answers, the implication that any challenge of their diagnosis or interpretation meant I was "in denial," and I resented learning that the experts were immune to questioning.

I was both frightened and angry with Tyler for the time all of this took, the trips to different hospitals, the family sessions, the constant surveillance, the worries and the time away from other obligations to talk and comfort, and perhaps, some part of me was angry with her for having any problem at all. Hadn't I always read to her and loved her and treated her with respect? How dare she do this to me? How dare she be miserable and make me miserable? How dare her life not turn out perfectly as I had planned?

Tyler has slowly crept out of her misery, anger and self-loathing. She is still fragile, and easily terrified, but her voice sounds connected to her core now rather than floating from her, untethered. Her lightness of spirit mingles well with her complicated, slanted, very layered view of the world, and her abundant, sometimes searing wit. She seems to have a tight but loving hold on herself. She has found a way to put the pieces of her life together to form a solid whole and to live within herself more fully rather than changing shapes to fit the demands of the moment. A couple of years ago she did a stunning performance of George Sand for the Chautauqua, and last year she was Annie Oakley. She sends Hudson, my grandson, videos she has made, complicated, funny, absurd and impressive in their professionalism. I don't really know if she could be the delightful, creative person she is now without her painful past, but how I wish, for both her and Kate, that they had not spent so many agonizing days and months, debilitated by self-hatred and drugs or alcohol.

I can look back now, after many years struggling to surface out of my own depression, and see how the importance of self-sufficiency and being "fine," tools I learned as a child, played a huge role in me not asking for help and being driven to succeed on my own, no matter how I felt inside. I can understand how the era in which I grew up lent itself to feelings of conflict and contradiction, and how the pressures to be all right and do it all led to a deep sense of dissatisfaction and disappointment. I cannot, however, understand how my daughters have not been able to push past the events or circumstances that could have contributed to their pain.

In Tyler's case, at least, I can draw a line between her feelings of inadequacy and depression and her father's abusive words and his cruel rejection of her. But I cannot grasp why Kate, who had her father's love and approval, no matter how far away we lived from him, who recalls her childhood as happy and full, could fall into such a dark hole of self-destruction. I want to find a reason to explain their difficulties or excuse the choices they made that were self-defeating and self-indulgent. However, I am still unsure if these answers exist, and, if they do, I don't know if they would provide any *real* clarity or comfort.

Just as I never imagined Tyler would grow into a woman whose life has been so burdened by her troubles, I felt the same bafflement as I watched Kate become caught in addiction, a world I had never known and could never have imagined her in. I came to understand addiction as sharing qualities with depression through my experience as the mother of a terrifyingly addicted daughter, first to drugs, and then to alcohol.

My feelings about Kate were less complicated than those I had about Tyler. Kate had never remembered her childhood as miserable. She didn't deny the privilege and the love and attention she got. But she stubbornly insisted on a life with drugs and wretchedness at its center, abandoning the enormous opportunities she had waiting for her. I was hurt and scared and sad, but I was better able to handle the self-blame and blame from others. My impulse to find a solution was not as interlocked with feelings of being held unjustifiably accountable. Those years with Tyler, and the little strength I gained through that, provided some support. But still I longed for Kate to be happy, to be healthy, to be whole, liberated from the fierce grip of her addiction. I ached from the awareness of how she was wounding herself, destroying her body and mind, ravaging her own spirit by feeding her demons. I had watched my sister suffer from alcoholism, go so low so many times that I could not imagine she could come up again, watched her pull herself laboriously out of yet another hole where she was almost buried by economic and physical loss. I dreaded to think of Kate following that path.

I am one of millions of parents who seesaw between hope and despair over their children and drugs. I replay the past, unraveling the things I did, didn't do, should have done and then conclude that they may well have not made any difference. Kate didn't suddenly rush headlong into hard drugs. She walked into them a day at a time, always testing the boundaries, drawn to the excitement of the forbidden or the unacceptable, rejecting anything that demanded hours, much less days, of commitment. She had been plagued since early childhood by intense feelings of despair and hopelessness over the enormity of suffering in the world. These could have been precursors of the images she could not rid herself of later; monkeys' heads being bashed against concrete, women with their babies slung to their bellies, forced to do pushups over water until they dropped and had to watch their babies drown, dead and mangled women in bushes and behind stores.

Whenever she saw a gruesome picture, read a newspaper article about genocide, watched a TV show depicting child abuse, or was confronted with real-life cruelty to animals or people, these images would become fixed in her mind. She would explain later that it was as if she somehow needed to actually *feel* how painful, how terrifying the experience was for the victim, and would recreate with precise details the horror of the event. At nine and ten she had marched with People for the Ethical Treatment of Animals (PETA) and demonstrated for animal rights time and again. By eleven she was fully committed to vegetarianism, then veganism, although I eventually forced her to eat fish and chicken because her early definition of vegetarian was heavy on breads, donuts and pastries mostly, some pasta, and very few vegetables.

I went to San Miguel de Allende in 2000 to spend my sabbatical. I wanted Kate to come there for Christmas. San Miguel was stunning at night, the colonial style buildings glowing under the starlight, the lanterns hanging from the balconies reflecting softly on the cobblestones, throwing shadows on the dusky adobe walls. I imagined we would walk to *el jardin* and she would delight in this new, more peaceful atmosphere. We would have Christmas Eve dinner at a small restaurant with colorful tablecloths and deep blue tile floors, warmed by a fire burning in the stone fireplace. On Christmas day, we would join friends in the most elegant restaurant in town, white tablecloths, lush paintings and plants in the open dining room, beautifully dressed people celebrating this day. My mother called me on Christmas Eve. Not having heard from Kate for several days, Tyler and my mother went to my house, using a key we had hidden to get inside. The house was empty and looked neglected, cold. Her room was a mess, clothes tangled on the floor, her things scattered and misplaced, and her bed was littered with a terrifying assortment of hypodermic needles and alcohol swabs stained brown with blood.

I thought, bright as Kate was, lovely and creative and funny as she was, she would get through the rough patches that began to show up in high school and on she would go. Her grades in high school reflected her attitude of indifference, rather than her ability or intellect. She was continually waiting until the night before a paper or project was due before she started her work, sometimes relying on her natural writing ability to get a passing grade and sometimes not turning in anything at all. In college she repeated her patterns of procrastination and avoidance, and soon was dropping classes. She moved out of the dormitory and in with her boyfriend and some other kids their age, and soon quit going to class altogether. I am unable to piece together a coherent timeline of her downward spiral, but soon she was almost a stranger to me. She could not stay committed to anything, unable to focus because she was either high for days at a time or coming down for days at a time. She got a few small jobs, keeping them for a day or a week, or never showing up. After moving to San Francisco, supposedly to find her calling and attend City College there, she eventually gravitated to a crowd of hard users, and solidified her life around drugs, falling in love with a thirty-five year old Iranian pusher, and moved with him into a weekly hotel on one of the roughest blocks in the Tenderloin.

The feeling must be incredible. Her life for the next two years was built around the next high and the feeling she got when she had it. I cut my sabbatical short and came home to deal with a problem that was to baffle and terrify me for years to come. My life was built around fear. I had days of hope, when she contacted me or I was able to track her down, but the overriding feeling was a clutching terror that she would die, either through overdosing or being shot by a dealer or someone else who was high. Short of that, I imagined she would never be drug free, and I put her face on every homeless, strung out young woman I saw on the streets. I didn't just *think* that could be her, I knew it would be her unless there were some way to change her path, and yet, at twenty-one, she was on her own. I talked to police in Reno and in San Francisco, and they were both understanding about my concerns, having heard them from hundreds or thousands of parents, and hopelessly unhelpful. They described meth users as the bottom of the barrel, the scum of the street, and yet, unless they found them breaking a law, they couldn't intervene. I thought that instead of jail, isolation on a farm or an island might be possible. I didn't think she was doing drugs because she was emotionally disturbed, but I knew she was emotionally disturbed because she was doing drugs. I had no control, no power, and

I hesitated to have her arrested and jailed, especially in California where I would not have access to her. Later, I realized the only solution *was* to have her jailed. She was unwilling to stay in a program that would help her get clean. She didn't want to get clean *really*; she just wanted to be left alone to do drugs.

I hatched all kinds of wild schemes with my family and friends. We would kidnap her, coax her into the car under the guise of going to lunch, then auto lock the doors and drive her to Reno, hogtied in the back between my daughter Tyler's husband, Shawn, and his friend, John, Tyler driving. Tyler went to Kate's room, room 604, Union Hotel, a weekly rental where you have to leave your identification at the front desk and only one person at a time can visit the room. Kate was taking a shower in a stall with a metal pipe pushing through the cracked wall. She was thin, her face marred by sores. She seemed agitated and was more eager to get Tyler out of there than she was happy to see her. The bed was strewn with drugs, packets of meth and cocaine, small bottles, some stacks of cash rubber-banded together. Tyler called me and insisted she couldn't leave her there. She would contrive some way to get her out, away from Ramón, and then force her into the car. Kate was defensive and self-righteous. She was great, drugs were great, she wished we could all do them together and that her Dad and I could get a grip about reality, let go and experience something out of our everyday world. Tyler talked Kate into calling me, and in the midst of the "fucking" this and the "fucking" that, it became clear that Kate was nuts about Ramón, the misunderstood and much maligned drug dealer, a loyal friend, not what we thought at all with our stereotypes and judgments. Besides, she assured me, he was going to give up the dealing, get a legitimate job as a bouncer, and she would get a job, just do drugs on weekends, maybe a little ecstasy at raves.

We spent more hours contacting police and district attorneys here and there. We discovered just what we could have guessed; there were thousands of kids on the streets in San Francisco doing just what she was doing. She was legally an adult, so if they arrested her she would go to jail, and if we got them to go to the hotel to arrest him, if she was in the room with drugs, she would be treated as a dealer too. The options were slim. We backed up. We called treatment programs, directors, drug and alcohol counselors, and heard the same conflicting messages over and over: "There's nothing you can do until she hits bottom and wants help," vs. "She needs your help and love and you need to force her into something before she dies." A friend looked up everything he could find on-line about methamphetamines and ecstasy and other drugs we suspected she was taking. He e-mailed me short messages: "Good Morning Sweetie, Here is an update on the drug situation—looks as if this addiction is worse than heroin—just thought I'd keep you informed," or "I talked to a lieutenant in San Francisco and he advises that if she is arrested they have first time offenders diversion programs, but after that she'll have a felony record." One of our friends whose son had been on drugs for two decades, advised: "If they're using and their lips are moving, they're lying—don't listen to them and do anything you can to get them in treatment." One friend had read that Angela

Lansbury had kidnapped her son and sent him to an island with no possible escape for six months and suggested we do the same. That sounded as good as anything else.

I was not telling my family or many other people about this in any detail in order to avoid their judgments, not only about Katie, but about me. What would you expect, single mother, "broken home," working mother, feminist mother. The last thing I wanted was to have some therapist talk to her about how she had been abandoned as a child, get her in group therapy where she would be encouraged, applauded even, as she could see how her addiction was really a result of a horrible childhood and a dysfunctional mother. I vacillated between trying to convince myself that she was a potentially normal twenty-one year old young woman, although temporarily living with a drug dealer in the Tenderloin rather than finishing her degree in anthropology, and that she was irrevocably addicted to drugs up to and including heroin and she would have to spend the rest of her life struggling in and out of treatment programs. I was sometimes afraid of Kate, of her violent rages and her strength, this same daughter who had been my little girl, happily splashing in the bathtub or leaning over to smell a flower in our yard, looking for Easter eggs, cuddling her animals.

I finally acknowledged that she was an adult according to the law if nothing else, and that I had absolutely no control over her life, even if she didn't either. I wasn't going to become my mother who had built too many of her days and nights around my alcoholic sister, vacillating between denial and enabling. I was solid in my knowledge that I was not to blame, and imperfect as I was, I was just as loving and caring a parent as thousands of parents whose kids weren't doing drugs. I never thought I would be worrying about this. She was supposed to be in college, studying, maybe with a little part time job, making plans to join the Peace Corps or travel for a year in Europe after graduation.

The trap of drugs is deadly for the user, and it destroys the rest of us too. For two years, my first thoughts every morning were about Kate. I woke up each night praying she was alive. I saw only bleakness in her future, and knew that I would never be able to unravel myself from the terrible loss if she died. I had watched my baby's first steps, and recorded her first words, winced as the needle sunk into her fat little bottom each time she got her inoculations. I collapsed into primordial fear and pain when I imagined my child, now a young woman, alone in her room on Christmas day, tying off her arm and plunging a needle into her vein.

I was not only scared, I was angry. Angry that I had worked so hard to do it all as a parent, to do the music lessons, the soccer, the horseback lessons and shows, the endless hours of reading or grading papers in a barn or the car while she practiced. I sometimes hated her for ruining my life, and wanted to discard her, to simply banish her from my life. I was angry that so much of my life had been built around her needs, and Tyler's. I thought birthdays and plays and performances and trips together and traditional holidays meant something. I couldn't understand how all of that had made no difference—I might as well have been a prostitute, lying drunk in bed all day, ignoring my children. Why had I bothered with all of that? What difference did it make to be there every night, to make a healthy breakfast every morning, to pack special lunches, to always think first about them and second about me?

I awoke one morning at 3 a.m. planning Kate's funeral. I had as a model the funeral of Tyler's brother, Sam. He was only two years younger than Kate. Kate had called me in Mexico, devastated by seeing Sam in his casket. She couldn't imagine the pain his mother was feeling and Kate's response was to just stand by her, listening to her mew quietly. Kate was stunned to see his mother taking photographs of the flowers, the guests, the church, and finally, of Sam. These would go in an album along with pictures of his first birthday and his graduation from high school, and they would help her see his life as meaningful. She would be able to hold his life more closely to her, find a way to make it mean something after finding him in the bathroom with a needle in his arm, the baby she had loved for only twenty years.

I began to revisit all the funerals I had attended—that of the toddler whose devastated mother backed over her on her tricycle in the driveway, of Robbie, my cousin, who was crushed when his mother's foot slipped from the tractor pedal as she reached down to scoop him up, of my friend's husband who died in the night of a heart attack, of a friend's son, only nineteen, who died on the tennis court of heart damage he had suffered as a child, and who refused to stop playing tennis and skiing with his friends. I found myself becoming resentful, insisting I would not invite friends who had not supported me during this time to her funeral, that I would bar Kate's friends who I suspected of doing drugs with her from the door, not tell her father or my brother because they would talk about God or God's will or blessings, and I would hate them for it. I would in fact only allow my mother, her sister and me in some bare room with her, knowing that we could not offer one another condolences, or hugs, but would keen and weep and slam things and tear at ourselves and accuse her and berate her and then deny that it had happened because we simply couldn't bear it.

I finally convinced her to come home. She came willingly, like she was being pulled not just by me, but by hope. She slept with me for the first few nights, very restlessly, jerking violently in the night and sleeping long hours at a stretch during the days. Slowly her skin got clearer, her eyes brighter, and she began to think about friends and food and books. Slowly we were able to talk about programs, and very slowly we could put together plans, many of which were ignored or broken in the days to come, but enough of which were pursued for us to piece together some time during which she could begin to decide what she wanted to do other than get high. A year later she still wanted to go back to San Francisco, and if Ramón had encouraged her, she surely would have. Maybe he loved her enough to know how terrible her life would always be with him, and he refused to have her back. For that I am appreciative.

The choices Kate had made for two years were deeply embedded in her history with drugs, with people associated with drugs, and by now, with her sense of herself. She soon slipped into doing drugs again. Perhaps she only felt like herself when she was doing drugs. Her identity was linked with drugs in many ways that reinforced her use. She felt a great deal of shame, defensiveness and anger. She felt that people identified her as an addict and she felt trapped by that identity. Her continued use reinforced their labeling of her, and she felt even further trapped, angry and hopeless. To what extent her need for drugs was physical I don't know. How her use began again, I also don't know. I have no idea what it felt like to her, or how it changed her thoughts. I do know that she was agitated and restless, unable to focus long enough to carry any action or thought through to completion. She was like a hummingbird whose wings are a blur of motion, even when hovering, almost frozen, over a bloom. What could I have seen earlier? What should I have done earlier? How would it have helped?

I began to think that my entire life had been wasted. Everything I had done had been pointless. I had put so much of my life on hold, convinced it was the right thing to do, and now I felt resentment and self-pity. I thought I was a careful, attentive and involved parent. I had gone through ten years of fear and blame with Tyler, from hospital to therapist, trying different drugs, worrying about her killing herself, and even at some point, when she was her most miserable, understanding why she might want to, and the idea of going through at least the next ten years living Kate's nightmare with her was unbearable. Tyler, I could understand more easily. Kate, I neither understood nor forgave. But, I got over the anger, the "after all I did for her, how could she?" and changed it to "I have done all I can for her, and now she can . . ." One day I was resolute and virtually blameless, determined to go on with my own life, convinced that Kate was the only one who could help herself, freed from self-blame and the tight ache of fear. The next day, I would sink again into despair and dread.

With enormous difficulty, and after many years, Kate was able to abandon methamphetamines. She went almost immediately to a complete and devastating addiction to alcohol. At first, so great was my relief that she was off drugs I refused to see her spiraling into another addiction. But after a terrible trip to Italy, a horrendous assault she survived after leaving a bar with two Italian men who locked her in a room and raped her, and a return to this country desperate for alcohol, I realized that she had not gotten clean, but had only replaced one addiction with another. I have, for the last several years, recognized that alcohol can be, and is for her, as devastating as drugs. She has gone through several treatment programs, jail, probation, meeting after meeting, therapy after therapy, narrowly escaping death in automobile accidents, and has by now struggled daily for almost half her life with the powerful hold that addiction has on her.

The struggles my younger daughter has fought with her own powerful demons continue today as she stacks a few sober months on top of a self-destructive, alcohol soaked week or month, each failure to maintain sobriety leading to a renewed commitment to sobriety but with an increase in self-loathing, hopelessness, and fear that she will be forever owned by her "obsession of the mind." I am terrified that she will lose the relentless struggle and end up frozen to death like Senator George McGovern's daughter, leaving her son with me, or worse, with his father. The only good thing to come of her alcoholism, as if one needs to find something positive, is that she has mined her horrific struggles for material that illuminates the complex underpinnings of the problem she faces, forging fantastic self-deprecating and cunningly accurate caricatures of alcoholics and drug addicts and their accounts from the hours and hours of AA meetings, treatment programs and therapy sessions she has attended. She would make a great stand-up comedian.

Today, and almost every day, even on the coldest days, Kate and I walk three or four miles. Now her baby, who we took turns pushing in his stroller, snuggled deep in the blankets, is almost four and points out the birds and horses and his friends' houses in our neighborhood, and tells jokes, plays ball and dresses himself. She sometimes still wakes with him at night, and comforts him back to sleep, delights in each new skill, and seems perfectly amazed that this wonder is her boy. And despite this deep love, this desire to forge a perfect life for herself and her child, it was only three months ago that she was in the hospital with alcohol poisoning and I was suddenly overwhelmed by the responsibility of being this baby's guardian, terrified by the possibility that I would be attending PTA meetings and soccer matches at seventy-five, completely missing what I thought would be a happy retirement, moving forward again as a "single mom," this time much older, much more tired, and broken by the loss of this daughter who owned one huge piece of my heart.

VII
Coming to Terms

The intricately beaded border of the Chiapas bracelet I bought in San Miguel de Allende is a deep ruby red, edged by a row of tiny pearl-gray beads, the wider part of the bracelet a series of light stars of a creamier gold, a small violet center, all woven together in a subtle mélange. The young woman who beaded it sat on the floor, her baby snuggled in the folds of her bright skirt, beading another pattern. We exchanged some pleasant words, I in my ragged Spanish, and I left wearing the jewel-toned cuff wrapped around my wrist, linking me to her and to this beautiful place. Because I am removed from the demands and familiarity of home, and am here long enough to make a home but not to build a life, time is more fluid and fuller. I am outside of myself here but not lost, consciously feeling a part of the stream of time that pulls me into its flow, merging me with others here. The demand to be visible, to be solidly formed in order to find appreciation, is largely missing, only reemerging for me in particular bars or restaurants.

My friends and I love the clothing shops and we buy beautiful things. We buy them because they are beautiful, because the fabrics and colors are beautiful, not because they will make us beautiful. Young and old alike stop and buy roses from the street vendors, and I begin to take for granted the smooth softness, the eager reds and quiet creams and yellows of these roses that are brought from the country-side every day. On many street corners vendors sell roasted corn on the cob dipped in butter or dusted with a soft, dry cheese, fruit drinks in plastic bags held together to form a neck at the top, plastic cups of pomegranate seeds, or nuts, or straw-berries, plastic sacks of watermelon slices, and cantaloupe and green melons. People eat on the street; the schoolchildren buy nuts and ices and puckered yellow chicken feet in hot sauce from vendors in the schoolyards during recess and after school. The old men who oversee the sorbets and fruit and roasted nuts make small talk with the children.

Time and place merge here. Age can begin to feel like a smooth and light time of life, a legitimate place to occupy in one's passage from birth to death, not an embarrassment or a shameful but unavoidable status. The generations meld more easily, even though the young people gather in the clubs and bars, the old people in their homes or at the park. All of the celebrations in *el jardin*, the central plaza in town, from the loud Parade de los Locos to the nativity celebrations, include babies, teens and old people. The day before I left San Miguel to return to the United States, a pilgrimage in honor of a saint began at the beautiful medieval Paroquia, as did so many celebrations. It included women in their eighties and pre-teens and their parents, all of whom set out to walk the thirty miles to Guanajuato.

North Americans are very separate from the Mexicans here, the poor and working class Mexicans as well as the very wealthy Mexican families who live in the stunning colonial homes or expansive ranches outside of town. Americans here are not striving, not competing, not trying to outdo one another or to race against the clock, or to build a nest egg or save to buy a house or car. These Americans are living on what they have saved, often supplemented by what little they earn within the expatriate and tourist community. They have exchanged their structured, demanding lives for this much simpler life of waking, working on whatever makes them happy, walking, eating, enjoying plays, and movies. Many of the women who live here have been away from the United States for thirty or forty years. They have traveled and lived for years at a time by themselves or with their children or lovers in Costa Rica or Guatemala or Jamaica and have supported themselves teaching English or giving haircuts or massages or lessons in photography or art. Most of the Americans here are nearer the end of their lives than the beginning, and can live with a great deal more grace and ease than they could if they remained in the United States. The benches in *el jardin* are the meeting place of the retired Americans who have come here to vacation or to live. They find their way along the rough cobblestones to the shops and services, take art classes and Spanish classes, and enjoy the delicious and often inexpensive food offered in the many restaurants.

Life here contrasts with the hard, striving, competitive lives we are so accustomed to living in the United States. Wonderfully generous and successful men I have known hammer away at themselves for not being more or doing more or having achieved more. Women struggle with work and family and relationships, often turning on themselves with criticism and denigration. Women often find themselves wanting in some way, never enough, or perhaps too much, so that there is no zone of comfortable acceptance. Women here seem willing to move past that self-judgment which almost always turns into condemnation and to view themselves as creators of a life that has meaning, as perfectly acceptable beings in a safe and accepting world. They are doing what matters to them, and in their activity, turn outward toward others or toward new places and interests rather than inward finding flaws and speaking of their inadequacies.

The women, mostly older, who have come to San Miguel, have constructed a social world in which they connect directly to one another, not to one another through the gaze of men. Women write or paint or photograph with their sights on what they can produce, or the process of creation. Having abandoned a place that values them so narrowly, they are not limited to discussions about their faces or bodies. Leaving behind their work, their families, and starting new in this new place, allows them to connect with their own wants. The armor of self-restraint and control gives way to a person more accepting of both imperfection and strength. Here, I do not search my face every morning for flaws, new signs of aging, and I do not see my body through condemning eyes.

Some cultures allow women to get old easily and early. They expect that when a woman marries and has children she will become physically larger, looser and more comfortable, that her body will expand as she expands to fit the larger demands the community assigns her as wife and mother. She is not expected to remain physically fixed, to *preserve* herself, to *maintain* appearances. She is expected to enjoy the freedom that comes with "letting herself go." Women's bodies are expected to change with maturity and particularly with childbearing, not only because the physical body stretches and expands, but because the self has expanded. From the thin light body of their girlhood, women gain substance and breadth as they assume responsibilities for their family and the community. Their bodies grow to accommodate their increasingly heavy responsibilities. Among some Native American tribes, a woman's body determines her status as married or unmarried. As she matures, she becomes full, ripe, broad, soft . . . she is expected to be able to persevere, to withstand and to be strong. She has the right to "throw her weight around." At the same time that she is expected to be nurturing and comforting and enveloping, her body is expected to change to reflect her role as nurturer and comforter. Childbearing and child rearing and survival require a woman to be strong, capable, and solid. A woman is not a girl. A woman is a grownup. And her body is not the body of a girl, who has experienced nothing. The experience of a woman is written not just on her face, but also on her body and she is allowed to relax into maturity and old age.

Here in the United States, on the other hand, women, especially in the middle and upper classes, are punished for "letting themselves go." Long after our childbearing years are over, and even after our children have left home, we are still to be lithe and girl-like, and to achieve that, we measure what we eat and condemn ourselves if we relax our grip on ourselves. It is important that we camouflage any flaws we cannot erase, flaws being any weight or wrinkle that reveals that we have a past. We must maintain our appearance, tighten, limit, make up for and make over, and in sum, pay more heed to how we appear than to how we are.

After so many years of lessons on the importance of how we look and present ourselves, not on what we feel and desire and want, this becomes almost natural. We learn to know ourselves in terms of these exterior qualities, losing touch with our feelings that are connected with an authentic deep self. Echoes from our mothers' voices and those we hear in coffee shops and at parties carry heavy warnings. "She has really let herself go since she got married," linked with "You cannot blame him for leaving her, she really let herself go after she had her last baby," serve as reminders of what could happen to any of us if we are not careful, vigilant. We are to keep a tight rein on ourselves, to keep up appearances, to control our weight and shape. The only thing worse than an angry woman in this society is a loose woman or one who is out of control as evidenced by some extra pounds.

What freedom to "let yourself go," to find power through loosening up, un-winding, abandoning the restrictions. Letting yourself go demands untying and unbinding the self, relaxing, freeing, and easing into something and someone larger. Women who are fat speak to us of woman's appetites, of desire and need. A fat woman is not easily owned by others, having a dark and powerful secret life, hidden from us but revealed in her hugeness. Having thrown off the restrictions of feeble femininity she can become a solid presence, someone to be contended with. No longer restricted by the demand for thinness, she can dive into her appetites; for food, for sex, for talk, for expression, for relationships. She can be less cautious, embrace her power, live large in the world. She is a dangerous woman. She is not kept in check by social disapproval; she may even be immune to condemnation— she may do exactly as she pleases rather than concern herself with pleasing others.

The restrictions on women's lives are reflected in the way we restrict ourselves. The approval of others is based so solidly on our appearance that our efforts are to shape ourselves into an acceptable form no matter how contrary that physical expression is to our psychological or emotional desires. If we can keep our bodies tightly circumscribed, we reflect the control we have over our appetites more generally. To refuse a luscious piece of chocolate cake is to refuse to give into our desire, to restrain ourselves for the approval of others, an indication of how important their evaluations are compared with our own internal desires. Our drives to expand, to take, to fill up space and to be free are curtailed by the social demand that we wrap ourselves tightly into our bodies, keep our legs crossed, our hands in our laps, our heads demurely tilted, our bodies not too firmly situated, not solidly grounded, but poised to move in the directions others, especially men, would want. Our bodies are trained to reveal our compliance and to deny our strength and independence, to reveal that we are aware of the narrow boundaries of our lives and to demonstrate that we accept them as legitimate.

We are required to watch our bodies, protect them from intrusion, exploitation, deterioration, and decline. We are to guard the perimeter. There are indeed exceptions, like Anaïs Nin, who was a peculiarly self-created woman, a "man's woman" who saw herself as born to please men. I have always had a difficult time understanding the appeal of Anaïs Nin, especially to feminists. Perhaps I can't get beyond her self-aggrandizing talk, her evident belief that she discovered sex, or perhaps her insistence on sharing the contrived minutia of her sexual forays, her sense that others would be enlightened and enhanced by being made privy to her peculiar obsession with her sexual life, but more likely it is that she would abort a fetus over six months old because it would interfere with her "calling" to be a sexual servant for men. But, what may appeal to the millions of women who have raved about her diaries, is that she is sexual, she uses her sex to have what she wants, she is not used, she is sexually powerful. While she may not have let herself go physically, she has let herself go sexually, risking judgments about appropriateness and self-control.

There is far more to aging than the process of biological change and social transformation. There is a deeply held evaluative component that we have all incorporated from a very young age, and when we become aware of ourselves as aging, we impose these heavy cultural judgments on ourselves. If we are valued primarily in terms of our bodies, our appearance, we, as women, have nowhere to go but down as we age. And accompanying that evaluation is a verdict on our self-worth. If we are not valued, than we are worthless. But there is more. We are symbolic to other women of what is bound to happen to them and they fear us just as we fear ourselves. We are revealing the underlying inadequacy of ourselves by aging and by having lost our ability to fill the social standard that allowed us acceptability. This has to stop. But for this to happen, constructions of value based on body have to change. If aging for women is mostly negative, it is because our value is so closely tied to our bodies, and no matter how many sentinels we place on guard around ourselves, our bodies change. Reconstructing aging as something other than loss depends on completely re-conceiving ourselves and it means taking the risk of being powerful in our own right, giving up the dream instilled so early and so well, that our power comes only from the men who desire us.

Oddly enough, despite the sense of diminishment or shame some of us feel as we age, women my age probably didn't grow up hating their bodies like many of our daughters did. Our models were fewer, more distant and we didn't think we would *become* them. We might have changed our hairstyle and worn tight black pedal pushers, ballet slippers and white shirts to look like Audrey Hepburn, but we were pretty clear on the difference between movie stars and ourselves. Models in *Vogue* or even in the *Sears* catalog, were still models. They were separate and distinct from us and our own lives, living in a highly romanticized, inaccessible world. But as we age, we have, like our daughters, begun to view ourselves in terms of our bodies, and like our daughters, we are deficient. We did, at least, have twenty or thirty years to enjoy our bodies, to make friends with them so that we can carry into our futures a past that was positive. I wonder about the young women who have despised themselves since they were eight or ten, those who dieted incessantly, who ran or threw up or took laxatives in their pursuit of a valued self through a perfect, but perfectly unattainable, body. Did they learn this too from mothers like me who were not willing to settle into being comfortable old mom, baking cookies and babysitting the grandkids, easing into a bigger dress size each year?

There is no real marker for being old like there is for being a teenager or an adult. Like many women, I still feel a startling disconnect between the woman who looks back at me when I glance into a store window, and the woman I thought was walking down the sidewalk. I began to realize that other people saw me as old, or older or aging, very slowly, the change almost imperceptible. The guy who came to measure the windows for new shades couldn't help but notice how pleasant and big the house was and offered that it was a great place for the grandchildren. At yoga class, the instructor approached me with concern, showing me how I could hold the poses in a way that was less strenuous, less physically demanding. I recently found myself slinking out of a bar that was full of young people, feeling foolish and wrong. How did this happen to me? When did I become old? But, more importantly, why and when did I become ashamed of being my age, of being older, of being old? What is shameful about that?

I don't really know what the specific signs of aging are—the hair, the body, the face? Is it the way I move or talk or some subtle combination of these? What is it, whether I'm dressed in jeans and a sweatshirt or dressed elegantly for the evening, that communicates to others "grandmother" or "old"? Is it something specific, or some blend of movement, appearance, and style? Or is it instead a withdrawal, a closing in on myself, and a self-protection that comes from not wanting to be found lacking? The more important question is why do I resist? I tune into people my age who are grandmothers and who still at least look as if they have some sexual selves—my ex-husband's wife comes to mind first—but I move on and find others . . . the checkout clerk at the grocery store, a professor in another department, a friend of my daughter's who is beautiful and bountiful and silver haired. They model aging comfortably and naturally, but that is my view, not necessarily theirs, and this is something we simply don't talk about.

I catch myself in the rear view mirror and insist that I get beyond the loose chin and the bags developing under my eyes. I cannot spend the next thirty years feeling loss and damage because I'm getting old, I tell myself. I need to have a bigger life than that. I am shocked and embarrassed at how I condemn myself for no longer being the woman men look at, after all those words about doing, not being, action, not passivity, the solo self, not the relational self. God knows, I always thought (and taught) that those lucky ones of us who had a career, who didn't build our lives on our looks, would sail into old age with glory and ease. I was wrong. How we age is tied more to the deep, meaningful connections we have with those we love or with consuming, rewarding work than to the mantle of achievement and success. The desire to be attractive, the feeling of inadequacy, can grab you just as hard if you are a doctor or lawyer as if you're working the night shift in a factory. What women *do* offers far less protection than to whom we are connected. This challenges the comfortable assumptions it was so easy to espouse at thirty. But what did I know about aging at thirty? Absolutely nothing and I knew almost as little at forty. But by forty, I was already aware of aging and of sometimes being overlooked, something that astounds me as I look at my splendidly beautiful forty-year-old daughter. This sense of loss is particularly ludicrous since most women I know hated being the object of male catcalls and wolf whistles. The objectification that accompanied them however, the suggestion of male power and privilege, are a training ground for the future: it is men who will approve, and then who will disapprove. We are to exist, be, for them, and then cease to really be when they no longer see us.

I was as surprised as anyone at the pain of suddenly being invisible, irrelevant. When I was young and almost by definition attractive, it was easy to dismiss the role that attractiveness played in my life because I could take it for granted and could emphasize the importance of other qualities. Little did I know that these other qualities were marvelous and sustaining as long as they were "add-ons" rather than replacements for the attractiveness. I won't go down this path like Germaine Greer, clamoring for women to achieve happiness and wholeness by becoming sexless old rags lurking about our gardens. Yet, I won't be stupid and resist reality. So, how between these two, do I find a way to look in the mirror every day and not feel loss?

I need to not look, to free myself from the power of the looking glass. But that is how we are shaped; through our reflection. We see ourselves through the eyes of others and given what we know about our culture and its values, we evaluate ourselves as we think others would. And any woman living in this culture knows implicitly what is valued, and she knows that her value as a full participant in the world diminishes as she ages. Her value can slide to grandmother or sweet little old lady but she is no longer taken seriously outside the realm of cooking or caring for others. Women know that their worth declines as they age, that their value is diminished with each year even as they also know that they can do more and be more, now than in the past. There is no room for aging. We feel the power of our loss when we are talking to a man whose eyes slide from our face at a party, whose glance settles not in our eyes, but in the room and faces beyond us. Within the punitive parameters of social acceptability we must find a way to value ourselves, whether that is completely isolating ourselves as some would suggest, abandoning ourselves as sexual and sensual people, people who want and need to be desired, or reframing and redefining our worth to allow us to embrace ourselves beyond our thirties.

All too often I see myself as old first, and then I find my other qualities. And this is what women have to move beyond—limiting ourselves to this sense of being nothing or "less than" because we are older. For women to contribute like we need to, to make our world or our own lives better, we need to gain strength from aging rather than define it as loss. And many women, women who have not worn the cultural hair shirt so close to their skin, have escaped the cultural dictates that would limit them so severely. These are women who can rely on their relationships, their families, and their value through their work, to build an identity separate from the heavy messages linking aging to loss. Both of my grandmothers and my mother carried a more substantial sense of their value with them into middle age than I have. They pulled on their deep roots in home, work, and family to do that. The solid expectation of being wives and mothers offered a strong foundation on which they built their worth, as they traversed the terrain from youth to old age. Youth, for them, was preparation, a brief passage to the real identity they assumed with marriage and family.

My grandmother White married a man she thought would allow her to escape the drudgery of her aunt's home where she spent her days working until nightfall, sleeping only to wake to more work. Her value came from being a mother, from being a competent farm wife, knowing how to plant and hoe and garden and can and freeze and make a home for her husband and seven children. On Sundays she put on a blue serge dress with a white collar or a dotted Swiss dress and wore a little rouge and lipstick, but her value did not lie in her appearance. She expected to fill out, to become matronly, to be "Mom" and, before long, "grandma," rather than to maintain the body or the identity she had before marriage. Her work, bearing and raising children, provided her with meaning, so as she aged, she was well valued by the many people in her world. She was the center of the life her children led, the focus, and the matriarch. Her opinions about choices and decisions were highly valued by her children and her disapproval was powerful even though any respect she got from my grandfather was grudging. Aging for her was first a process of gaining status, and then, as she was older, freedom. She spent the last twenty years of her life feeling valued, happy, worthy, and none of this was dependent upon her good looks.

My mother's mother, Inez, loved my grandfather when they married, and loved him all her life, her value coming from having a lovely and welcoming home for their friends, her role as the wife of a highly regarded man, and from her children. While she was always considered a pretty woman, becoming an adult was accompanied by natural and expected physical changes . . . one's body changed, one put on weight, wore corsets and girdles to capture and contain the inevitable sags and looseness that accompanied childbearing. But these changes weren't devaluing; they identified my grandmother as a wife and mother rather than a girl, and they brought with them privileges and status that she had hoped for before she married.

When my parents divorced, my mother moved to San Francisco. At fifty, she wanted to be more than the mother of five children and my father's ex-wife. She wanted to leave the confines of those roles and be seen for herself. I remember understanding that on one level, and feeling a sense of deep rejection on the other. I had just had my first child and I wanted her to be "The Grandmother." She lived in San Francisco for over twenty years, building friendships and a very successful business, and in her mid-seventies she returned to Reno, but she still refused to be limited to grandmother. She loved her grandchildren but she insisted on being more; a political activist, a gardener, a friend. She did not long for a sexual relationship, realistically surveying the available men and rejecting a future which would almost without a doubt be absorbed by caring for a sick or dependent old man.

My mother has never hated her body, nor has she ever judged it harshly, even when she was in her eighties. She appreciated her strength, her ability to garden and walk and go wherever she wanted. She was careful about her health, and cared for her appearance; she saw her body as a friend and appreciated her good relationship with it. As a teenager, she was tall and slim and her concerns were with books and friends and school and art, and not for her body. She neither condemned her body nor particularly appreciated it. She accepted it and viewed herself as being far more than her body. Aging was movement forward, change, becoming *more* to herself and to others, not diminishment.

Even as Alzheimer's began to own her, she was thankful for the blessing of each day. She felt increasingly free to pull her past into her present. Her yard and garden reminded her of the house she grew up in, and her fruit trees reminded her of towing a wagon heavy with cherries and peaches up and down her street, trying to sell the fruit to her neighbors. Just last summer, she pulled her car to the curb, overcome by the beauty of *Swan Lake*. These memories remain, linked with the unravelling pieces of her past, as she now travels between girlhood and old age, comfortably settled in neither. Even so, when I, or any of her children, visit her, which we do every day, she fills our time together with outpourings of love for us and happiness that she has us, a deep joy in her family and her good fortune.

Why is our perception of aging so often one of loss? Clearly, we may become more physically frail in some ways, but in others we are less physically vulnerable. We are less likely to be killed in an auto accident, to be killed in a homicide, to be beaten by a loved one. We are immune to many illnesses, and we generally put ourselves less at risk in the world. We have had more experience, more education, more lovers, have seen more movies, and gone on more trips and just done more overall than when we were younger. Why is all of this not something that makes us more? Why does age instead result in our deterioration? As years are added, why is the cumulative effect not grander than it is?

My daughters and I had lunch together recently. I sat with these two beautiful and warm young women, women I love deeply and with great pride. I nonetheless bridled at being replaced by them, disappearing into just their mother and losing me, Mary. A friend of theirs came up to our table and greeted them both by name and then, to me, said warmly, "and how's lovely mother?" I am their mother. I *love* being their mother. I adore my daughters. Yet, being transformed into "mother" made me feel finished. I have seen this happen to my own mother and to other women, and while it causes pain, they, and I, maneuver carefully through our feelings so that our tender bonds with our daughters are not bruised or broken by these judgments.

Of course there were always women who identified as witches or crones, particularly during the late 1970s and 1980s, ceremonially embracing man-free, goddess identities. These women were able to let go of the standards for femininity in our culture altogether while embracing a womanhood that was authentic, expansive, and completely woman-identified. Or so it seemed. But it also seemed to demand giving up too much of the self that I had grown accustomed to. The desire to be viewed by men as desirable, as sexy and attractive, was too central to my identity to simply walk away from it. One reason I found Germaine Greer's book, *The Change*, so disturbing was that she was willing to abandon, in fact was luxuriating in the abandonment of, the essential feminine self, the one that drew on male culture for its worth. While I might admire that on an abstract level, applauding the strength and richness she suggested we would gain from no longer having to relate to men, losing my thirst for their appreciation of me would be no easier than dealing with that loss. Greer was claiming, really embracing, the right to give up something that we were already losing. I still wanted to stay in the game, despite the fact that the cards were increasingly stacked against me. She could acknowledge the reality and withdraw from the competition, and redefine it altogether whereas my friends and I were playing 'til the last buzzer.

I didn't want to withdraw from men, to not have them in my life. I wanted them to grow up along with me, to not have such narrow standards, to get beyond seeing only a body or a face. I know the sociobiological perspective that holds that men are attracted to younger women and need to have indiscriminate and frequent sex in order to spread their seed as widely as possible, assuring the survival of the species. They're just doing their job. But that way of understanding attraction leaves a whole lot out, including the myriad ways we have sex with one another that have nothing to do with procreation and everything to do with what feels good. I wanted men to want me. But honestly, I wanted that in the abstract. In real, everyday life, most of the men I knew were not that interesting nor were they men whose company I sought, and they were probably a lot better off with a woman who would not expect much of them. Maybe wanting them reflected the power of cultural assumptions about being incomplete alone, needing a man not so much for who he was but for the legitimacy he brought with him. The message that women are unavoidably inferior unless claimed by a man, that women can be cleansed by a man, made acceptable to themselves and others through his acceptance, is a message both strong and wrong. Women know this full well. We sometimes want to be with a man at art openings or the movies not so much because we enjoy him, not because we want to be with that particular man, but because we know that being with a man communicates that we are normal, acceptable, and real. I think many of us struggle with this; wanting to be fine on our own, knowing we are smart and capable, yet having learned so well and so deeply that we are not enough alone.

Clearly not every woman fears aging, some, even in the United States, welcome the freedom and comfort it can bring. I suspect that women who are involved in completely rewarding relationships with men, or women, are much more comfortable with the process. These relationships are key—they validate us and give us the freedom to move more easily in our worlds. It's strange, counter-intuitive, that being alone, which sounds like it should offer more freedom and fewer constraints, actually can be limiting. This happens when we have learned the cultural lessons about our value coming from being chosen, being loved, but these messages are so strong we cannot deny them. And clearly most of us have lives that are occupied by things other than concerns about aging. But, when we pull aside the curtains that drape the structure on which self-worth and value are built, for many women, no matter how successful in other arenas, there lurks an unwelcome, insistent drone of loss and discomfort huddled in the weakened arms of aging.

Several years ago I spent a weekend at Pyramid Lake, by myself, in a small trailer. I woke to the glassy lake each morning and simply walked, read and rested for two days. On Monday, in the late afternoon, I returned to town and to my work and family. Driving to town, deep shadows bruised the soft hills purple and indigo. My skin welcomed the light dry breezes that ruffled through the open windows of my car. I had dinner alone in a quiet place, a glass of red wine, crusty bread and a simple meal made special as much by the surroundings as the spices, easing my way back into everyday life. Afterwards, I went to hear an old poet read her work. I wanted to be moved, buoyed, or even calmed by her stories. I don't remember her name, but her message disturbed me for years.

The poet's lines were limp and full of dreary stabs at the ordinary lives of women. Initially bland and murky, her poems soon revealed her blanket rejection of herself and of women in general. To a room full of women, she spoke of her deep dissatisfaction with being a woman and relentlessly demeaned the secrets and hopes of women, resentful of being sought rather than being the seeker. For her, the remedy for the inadequacy of the self was to merge with a man. The celebration of womanhood I had expected was instead a denunciation of the idea of women as powerful, whole or even adequate by themselves. Women were "the other" not because they were not men, not standard, not acceptable, as Simone de Beauvoir would have said, but because they were essentially inferior. Their character was defective and they could only be hoisted out of their innate mediocrity by a man. The poet spoke of men's secrets, always weightier than women's, of men's expressive and open lives compared with the dark, interior lives of women. This old woman had grown up with her mother and sister, three witches despised and taunted by their neighbors. This hatred she experienced settled within her own heart and relentlessly attacked her, shredding her self-worth, replacing it with loathing, a self-hatred eased only by the acceptance of a man. Only her connection with him gave her value.

I drove home through the heavy night, thoroughly diminished in spirit, reviving only partially when I walked in my door, welcomed by the warmth and lightness of my home, and the things in it that reflected me. I may need to ask myself why I rail against this notion that women are nothing alone. Is it not true that all of us want connection, relationships, is not every religious and media directive telling us that two make a whole, that one is incomplete, that our lives should be spent finding the one we will love and who will love us, that we will then be real and happy? I am probably like most women in wanting to love and be loved, to not be alone, but I am also like many in wanting to be seen and heard and appreciated, not judged and found wanting. And these wants are experienced at a time during which women struggle to convince themselves that they are more than a body, more than appearance, and yet know that they operate in a culture in which they are still mostly this. Opportunities we have gained during the last several decades are built on a base that threatens to crumble under the weight of deep and disturbing contradictions, contradictions that reflect both enormous progress and powerful historical pulls.

In *Mirror, Mirror*, Elissa Melamed, a wonderful woman, lush in body and spirit, wrote about the shame of getting old, admitting we were no longer the acceptable standard, not holding up our end of the bargain, which was that we would always be attractive. She wrote that we were allowed in the social world only so long as we did not reveal the dirty little secret of our physical humanity, only so long as we could help men maintain their fantasy about us and our purity and innocent beauty. When we got wrinkled or flabby or lost a breast or our hair turned gray, we revealed the secret of our debasement. Elissa Melamed died when she was only fifty-six, yet she could write knowingly of the feelings and experiences I would have in my sixties. It was the beginning of the long slide. I wanted to keep the woman who was able to be other things because she was first and foremost young and fairly attractive, but I met the ghost of the future who promised invisibility and loss as a woman, diminishing the value of my other accomplishments because they could not replace that loss. She was right: "Men look at themselves in the mirror. Women look for themselves."

Even if we think we are more than our looks, that we have talent, intelligence and a great education, we still have to get through that transition from being young and attractive to being old and, by definition, unattractive. As Elissa Melamed said, women often feel shame at being old, at no longer being a person that men want to look at. Marilyn French in *My Summer with George* expresses well the fear and cowardice that accompany getting old: "But mainly I dreaded being perceived as acting flirtatious or seductive toward anyone who might find my no longer young person repulsive. So afraid was I of finding my physical being a source of repugnance that I simply erased the young from my sexual vision . . ." If we assume that the other will be revolted or will stereotype us, we become inhibited, frozen. If we know they are judging us as unacceptable, we are not our best selves. If we are trying to hide a stringy neck with a turtleneck or a carefully placed hand, or by making sure we are not being viewed from the side or in full light, our interactions are contrived and our willingness to be visible, to be seen and heard, is inhibited.

While it may be true that we don't want to be old, it is more likely that we don't want to *look* old. There are some things we look forward to, especially as we get older, such as travel or leisure time or the freedom of not working and not being responsible for other people. Do we want to go back to college, to breast-feeding, to being poor, to proving ourselves at work? I think there is much about aging we like, but we know that our value to others declines. While we have more freedom and more opportunity, we know others see us as having less; less value, less attractiveness, less sexuality. We cannot escape the glance of the other. We have internalized the cultural gaze to such a degree that the other need not even be present. We take in our cultural values and judgments with each of our breaths, and become inseparable from the culture that forms us.

Women's efforts to change ourselves, through therapy or dieting or surgery, to make up for being female, and particularly for being an aging female, narrow our attention, link us too closely with our bodies, and constrict our power. Yet, the contradiction built into this is that if we are to retain sexual power, or social power, we have to be seen and heard, and for this we must be visible. Young women, attractive women are visible; old women are both invisible and mute. So, the manipulations of the self, altering the body's geography, creating a landscape on which women can build some strength, even as they capitulate to the cultural dictates that erase their intrinsic human worth, makes sense. We often treat our body like an enemy country. We declare war on it, we attack it, we brutalize it, change its geography, redraw its boundaries, alter its terrain, even when we are young, but especially as we age. Our relentless vigilance is rewarded only temporarily because we inevitably reveal the dirty little secret that we are no longer young, no longer valuable. Aging compromises our sexuality and because our value, actually our definition of self, is immediately tied to our sexuality, it is necessarily eroded as well. Of course men lose value as they age, particularly as they become infirm, but men become "old" much later, have far more latitude, and as long as they have power, either physical or economic, their masculinity is protected. I recently read a newspaper article about "young male politicians," all in their forties and fifties. It would have been absurd to read about "young women" in their forties and fifties, politicians or not.

Some women who have built themselves on achievement and work turn their considerable abilities on themselves, approach themselves as an object to be improved through hard work and sacrifice, so that their value holds. Others, familiar on an intimate basis with the nuances of power and value tied to their sexuality, carefully and thoughtfully navigate the construction site of their body, forming themselves into acceptable shapes accompanied by agreeable postures to maintain value in a world that values them only tentatively, temporarily, and only within very narrow limits. This process is clearly reactionary rather than reflecting comfort with a changing identity.

Some might suggest that aging is by definition loss because it leads to the ultimate loss, death. We may fear and shun all the indicators of aging because we know that every door we open onto a new year brings us closer to the final exit. After adulthood, especially middle adulthood, we begin to see our lives from the perspective of the years we have left rather than those we have lived. But I am convinced this is not the reason aging is so painful for us. Death is frightening to most of us no matter what our age. Death is a possibility at any moment; high school football players die on the field, children die in car wrecks, friends drown at swimming parties or giving birth, or have heart attacks at forty-five or fifty. Death is an abstract for many of us, a fact that has settled somewhere deep in our unconscious and lies there mute and invisible most of the time. We know it will happen to us, we know it will happen to our parents, and our friends, and even to our children. We could not live if we embraced the magnitude of that loss every moment. We keep it at bay through avoidance, humor, spirituality, work, or any number of less healthy ways.

Our fear of aging is a fear unto itself, unrelated to the inevitability of death. There is no shame in death; there is shame in getting old and being old. There is little effort to fool death; we know death cannot be fooled. We change our hair color, or have a face lift, or diet, not to avoid death, but to avoid looking old. The question for us is not how do we age gracefully, but how do we age happily and with vigor and pride and fullness? How do we maintain good feelings about ourselves, not shrink when we are in a crowd of thirty-somethings, not feel like a has been or a hag? How do we spend our future years not avoiding ourselves or being ashamed of ourselves because we are aging? How do we live well if we believe that we have already walked through all of the good moments in our life, and are now simply riding out an interminable decline? Really, ultimately, how do we retain our power?

A woman who is applauded, who is appreciated, is a woman who can act effectively, a woman who is heard is one who will talk, a woman who is appreciated for her sense of humor can be funny, and a woman praised for her beauty can use her body freely, openly and in a way that brings pleasure to herself and to another. But a woman who is not seen or heard loses her voice, her right to occupy space, her words are drawn back into her as they are ignored by others, and her body becomes only an encumbrance, wrong for the occasion and encouraging her to withdraw or diminish herself so as not to intrude on the space of other, younger women who deserve their place in the room.

To succumb to an ideology that erodes the landscape of the self to the point that a thin veneer of flesh stands for the whole of one's identity is destructive and intolerable. The glances that slide over one's face to others, the handshake accompanied by the eyes searching the room, the abandonment of even the semblance of polite conversation, lead to woman's diminishment of herself. Any child who is treated as worthless, as unimportant, as ugly or stupid will struggle with feelings of self-loathing all their life. In exactly the same way, because we are such social creatures, any woman treated as worthless not only turns on herself but finds herself turning away from her world. If others no longer listen, she no longer has anything of value to say; if they no longer see her, she no longer makes herself visible. Others' avoidance and diminishment of her make her disappear and she is ultimately lost to herself.

A woman must figure out who she is if she is no longer there in the eyes of others. If she becomes invisible, is not reflected back by others, thereby disappearing, is this only loss or is there something to be gained through what might feel initially like emptiness? Living decades alone, often more than half our lifetimes after our children are grown if we have them, or our marriages are over, cannot simply be endurance. These are not simply years of decline or loss, nor are they lives in which we can live through the accomplishments of our children. They are more. They are, just as author Carolyn Heilbrun says, "the last gift of time" and a gift that we are in a unique position to appreciate. If we are to be old at only fifty in our culture, we can have thirty or forty more years of living as outsiders, or we can abandon the truths with which we entered this part of our life and make it anew.

The struggle to see yourself when others are not seeing you is a difficult one. Years ago, my aunt, then about fifty-five, came to my house for coffee. She was visibly disturbed. She had earlier been in line waiting to be served and the clerk looked "right through her" to the younger woman behind her. She was very angry about being "invisible." I, at thirty-five or so, had not yet had that experience, but by now I have had it several times, and I know the humiliation and anger it provokes. Why shouldn't one be seen at every age? Why do so many of us denigrate ourselves, judge ourselves as less, step back, and out and away as we age? Why not stay in there, maintain our visibility, assert ourselves? There is no shame to this. But women feel that they have let themselves down, or let others down by getting old, by revealing who they really are underneath all the contrivances.

If women learn from childhood on to "be" rather than to "do," to be chosen rather than to choose, to wait rather than to take the first step, they are clearly ill prepared for aging. The invisibility that women often feel has far reaching consequences. Just as women misplace any political power they might have when they direct all their attention to their looks, when women are invisible to others, their power to act in the world is diminished. We learn early and well the loss that comes with age, and when we are the loser, the power and strength and presence we had are gone. We learn to take ourselves as a joke; to not take ourselves seriously in hope that we will still be allowed to at least watch the game.

Maybe there *is* some freedom in being invisible. Maybe there is some freedom on this side, where no one sees. But how can you see yourself if you are not there in the eyes of others? We cannot move as gracefully over the dance floor if our body is stigmatized, nor can we capture the room with our words if we know no one is listening. To exist, to maintain ourselves, we must find ourselves in the eyes of others, if not at the moment, then through the cumulative experiences we have gathered and can offer ourselves and others. If we believe aging to be shameful, to be ugly, something to be hidden or denied, then our bodies and our words reflect our belief in our own diminishment. Our maneuvers to hide our age are themselves constraining, we are sabotaged by our own efforts to hide ourselves, to conceal our reality in order to be acceptable.

In all of this discussion about invisibility and shame, about the consequences of not being seen or heard, there is a rock bottom assumption that unless a woman is seen or heard by a man she is not seen or heard at all. This gnashing of teeth over losing value and losing identity with age reflects purchase of the omnipresent social values that link a woman's worth to a man's evaluation of her, not a specific flesh and blood man necessarily, but the heavy weight of male values and male culture.

That is, it represents the oppressiveness of the male gaze. Reclaiming the gaze as your own re-establishes power and self-worth and an ability to move freely and effectively and unapologetically in the world. Why would one slink out of a bar because she had ventured into a place full of young people, marking her automatically as worthless, if she had not adopted the male gaze, the dominant evaluation? Why would she feel out of place at a party, unappreciated because she was unnoticed, apologetic for not having a man in her life, if she had not internalized the heavy denigration of women alone?

We must turn the gaze away from the self, look out rather than in, use our own eyes rather than seeing ourselves through the eyes of others. Walking the path through the quiet lushness of Loose Park last summer, I was struck by what I can only think of as the ability to see, to see out. I was able to acknowledge the power of my own sight, my own vision or view, in a very literal sense. The trees led my eyes to the turn of the century apartment buildings grazing the hill, and closer, the stately homes resting on sweeps of emerald lawn, and I was struck by the *seeing* of these things, with them being out there, accessible to me. I was looking out. That meant I was the source, the power center, the subject of my life rather than the object. Women do not have to abandon their sexuality and their power if they can center their identity in themselves instead of in others, particularly in the acceptance and approval of a man. However, this requires a real separation of the self from the assumed judgments of those others, an ability to see the self standing on its own, even while surrounded by hurtful cultural messages about women and aging, hearing those messages, knowing how to speak that language, but rejecting the dominant interpretations.

Coming to terms with aging means acknowledging the power of those gender messages that dampen and belittle while embracing, holding dear, those that celebrate, those that push you out rather than turn you in on yourself. It is a willingness to let go, to know you can't have it both ways; you cannot live deeply and with freedom and still desire approval by the world that forces you to take shallow breaths, to hold yourself in lest you make too much of yourself.